AN ASTROLOGER'S JOURNEY

MY LIFE WITH THE STARS

Paula,
always
enjoy playing
golf with you —

Kelly

ABOUT THE AUTHOR

KELLY LOWE is an astrological counselor, teacher and author. Her expertise lies in helping her clients understand themselves better and cope with difficult cycles in their lives. Timing is everything, and the use of astrology can be instrumental in selecting the right time to accomplish your goals. She has been studying and practicing astrology for thirty years. A past president of the *Astrological Research Guild*, she has taught astrology at Seminole State College and Daytona State College, and studied ancient astrology on the Greek Isle of Kos. She also gives frequent astrological lectures throughout Florida. She has appeared on national television and has been a regular guest on several radio shows.

Kelly publishes a monthly astrology newsletter which is available at her website, ***www.astrologytalk.com***, or sign up to receive it directly via email by contacting the author at Kellylowe@astrologytalk.com.

AN ASTROLOGER'S JOURNEY

MY LIFE WITH THE STARS

Kelly Lowe

CHB MEDIA, PUBLISHER

Library of Congress Control Number: 2011941531

ISBN-13: 978-0-9822819-8-7

CHB Media, Publisher
3039 Needle Palm Drive
Edgewater FL 32141
(386) 690-9295
CHBmedia@gmail.com

www.chbmediaonline.com

First Edition
Printed in the USA

Contents

PART I LEAVING PORT
Why I Went ... and Just Kept Going

PART II SHARING MY JOURNEY ...
And Making the Most of Life

INTRODUCTION

For thousands of years people have used the principles of astrology to help chart the course of their life's journey. In those early years when America was born, Thomas Jefferson and Benjamin Franklin "looked to the stars" for advice on when to schedule the signing of the Declaration of Independence. But the truest proof of astrology's influence is the overwhelming number of people who to one degree or another make astrology part of their daily consciousness. The two most frequently searched subjects on the internet are sex and astrology.

In Kelly Lowe's entertaining story, *An Astrologer's Journey*, the author comes to astrology like most people, looking for someone and something to help solve the puzzle of her life. But for Kelly it becomes the moment of departure on a long voyage. Astrology becomes her lifelong journey and her profession. She sails life's seas with passion, joy and sincere kindness, and inspires many people to put their trust in her as an astrological counselor.

An Astrologer's Journey is subtitled *My Life with the Stars*, and that's exactly what it is—a warm-hearted story, not a text on astrology. You don't have to "speak astrology" to enjoy it, although you'll come away with a deeper understanding of how the forces of the Sun, Moon and planets affect your life. So come on board and experience the inspiration in these pages. We are happy to have you along for the ride.

Bon Voyage!
Gary Broughman
CHB Media, Publisher

Gratitude and Appreciation

My heartfelt thanks to Brenda Brush who planted the seed thirty years ago which inspired me to make this journey; to my special friend Betty Riley for her vision and encouragement which inspired me to continue on my journey; and to Krista Ghaffarian for her support and efforts in helping me share my journey through this book.

Thank you to my family, friends and clients who have opened their hearts and shared their lives and experiences with me. They have enriched my life and helped make my journey so rewarding.

Special thanks to the very gifted and talented Gary Broughman, my collaborator, editor and publisher for his guidance, patience and direction. He was the catalyst in helping me communicate my dream of sharing my journey with the stars.

I want to especially thank my wonderful husband Tony. Without his love and support this book would not have been possible.

It is my sincere desire that you read this book with an open heart and an open mind. After all, "life's a journey—enjoy the ride!"

THE LANGUAGE OF ASTROLOGY, ABRIDGED
WORDS TO GUIDE YOU ON KELLY'S JOURNEY

(IF YOU ARE UNFAMILIAR WITH THE LANGUAGE OF ASTROLOGY, YOU MAY FIND THIS BRIEF "GLOSSARY" HELPFUL.)

Your Chart – Everyone has one. Your astrology chart is the picture of the sky at the moment and place you were born. It speaks volumes about who you are. If you don't like your chart and always wished you were born under a different sign, blame your parents—or the stars—not your Astrology Counselor.

Natal Planet – Where a planet was at the time of your birth, not the planet on which you were born. Most of us were born on earth, and those who weren't usually won't admit it.

Let Your Sun Sign In – Your Sun sign refers to the sign of the zodiac that your Sun was in at the moment and time of your birth. Your Sun sign describes your personality. If you don't like your personality, you can't hire a lawyer and change your Sun sign like changing your name. My advice is don't fight it, use it. There are wonderful possibilities in all the signs.

Aries – pioneering, independent, competitive, intolerant, aggressive

Taurus – patient, steadfast, conservative, materialistic, thorough

Gemini – literary, versatile, adaptable, analytical, curious

IX

Cancer – self-sacrificing, receptive, cautious, reserved, persevering

Leo – commanding, generous, ambitious, optimistic, opinionated

Virgo – ingenious, witty, studious, methodical, skeptical

Libra – persuasive, tactful, intriguing, undecided, judicial

Scorpio – secretive, penetrating, intellectual, investigative, temperamental

Sagittarius – jovial, progressive, philosophical, frank, zealous

Capricorn – laborious, forceful, scrupulous, thrifty, domineering

Aquarius – inventive, intellectual, diplomatic, independent, humanitarian

Pisces – intuitive, compassionate, introspective, loquacious, clairvoyant

My House or Yours – Understanding the houses in your chart takes you deeper into the language of astrology. Have you heard it said that accidents often happen in your own house? Well, good things happen there too. Knowing your chart can help determine how your story plays out.

In Western Astrology the astrological chart is divided into 12 houses. A house is an arc in space that represents 30 degrees. Hence, 12 houses equals 360 degrees. Each house represents an area of your life. And each house has a ruling planet, which is also known as a correlating planet ruler. I know that's a lot to grasp, but remember this: The houses tell us **"where"** something is going to happen.

1st house: Aries, Mars—your physical body

2nd house : Taurus, Venus —your finances and values

3rd house: Gemini, Mercury—your education and the way you communicate

4th house : Cancer, Moon—your home and family

5th house: Leo, Sun—your children, your love life, and your creativity.

6th house: Virgo, Mercury—your health and your work environment

7th house: Libra, Venus—your marriage or partnerships

8th house: Scorpio, Pluto—your sex life, inherence and joint finances

9th house: Sagittarius, Jupiter—your higher education and philosophy

10th house: Capricorn, Saturn—your career and public image

11th house: Aquarius, Uranus—your hopes, goals, dreams and wishes

12th house: Pisces, Neptune—your subconscious attitudes

Ascendant – Your ascendant is the Sun sign that was on the horizon at the moment and place that you were born. It is referred to as your "window to the world." If your Sun sign doesn't seem to completely describe you, peeking out "your window" might help you see your world more clearly. Don't be afraid to look. What you see might be a pleasant surprise.

Transits – Planets are always on the move. Transits are the constant rotation of the planets as they orbit the Sun. As they enter a house they tell us "**when**" something is going to happen. This is especially obvious when following the transit of the Moon. If you unexpectedly find your-self falling in love, and you're not dancing the *bossa nova* or drinking margaritas, it may be the Moon to blame.

Aspect – refers to the relationship or distance of one planet from another. The aspect of planets acting together can alter or increase their individual influence. We begin to see there's more to the language of astrology than just knowing the difference between an earth sign and a water sign. Astrology counselors train many years—and some-times shed many tears—before beginning their practice. So ... if you are an amateur sitting at home trying to ren-der your boyfriend's chart ... well, let me just say we don't want anyone getting hurt. And finally ...

Planets in Action — In the language of astrology the Sun and Moon are both planets, no matter what your 8th grade science teacher might say.

Sun – your inner being

Moon – your emotions

Mercury – you mental perception

Venus – your attitude about love and your self worth

Mars – your energy level

Jupiter – your guardian angel

Saturn – your tester and teacher

Pluto – your transformer

Uranus – your intuition

Neptune – your compassion

Elements — Each Sun sign is assigned an element which helps describe its characteristics. The elements are Fire, Earth, Air and Water

AIRES, LEO AND SAGITTARIUS are the *Fire* signs—known for their feisty high spirited energy.

Gemini, Libra and Aquarius are the *Air* signs—known for their mental and intellectual equity.

Taurus, Virgo, and Capricorn are the *Earth* signs—known for their logical, concrete and practical nature.

Cancer, Scorpio and Pisces are the *Water* signs—known for their sensitivity and keen intuition.

Part I

My Journey with Astrology

Why I Went ... and Just Kept Going

"There is only one success:
To be able to spend your life in your own way."
~ Christopher Morely

"To everything there is a season,
and a time to every purpose under the heaven."

~ Ecclesiastes 3:1

CHAPTER ONE

HELP WHEN WE NEEDED IT MOST

RELYING ON THE STARS

In November of 2010, two weeks before his birthday, my husband Tony was diagnosed with small bowel cancer, which we learned is very rare and very aggressive. Most people have never even heard of it. There are only about two thousand of these cases diagnosed each year in the United States. In most cases it is discovered when it is too late. The survival rate is less then fifty percent.

I couldn't help reflecting back to when my husband Larry had his fatal heart attack and wondering if I was going to be a widow again.

Surgery was scheduled within three days of when the cancer was diagnosed. Fortunately he had a wonderful surgeon who told me after the surgery that he had gotten it all. But it was very aggressive and had almost penetrated the wall of his small intestine. In another two weeks it could have been fatal. The doctor felt that we should follow up with a visit to an oncologist for treatment.

My heart sank. I could not believe that this was happening to us. It was almost the worst day of my life. The first worst day was the day that my father was diagnosed with lung cancer. He died six weeks later. So naturally, I was reliving this whole scenario all over again in my mind.

So we made an appointment with the oncologist. The doctor's recommendation was to begin chemotherapy as soon as my husband recovered from the extensive surgery he had just gone through to remove the cancer. He explained the severity of the situation. Although the surgeon had removed all of the cancer, there was still a risk that it could metastasize some place else in his body. He felt that my husband's probability of survival would increase if he chose to have the chemotherapy. So we had a decision to make that others before us also had faced: chemo or no chemo?

This may sound like an easy enough decision; you do everything they say you should do. You don't take risks. If chemo can increase your chances, you do it. Right? But the side effects they described were beyond tough. Brutal would be a better word. We knew that they always tell you about the worst cases, but still, it was a big decision to make.

It was right about this time that I was teaching an astrology workshop at the Daytona Beach Yoga and Wellness Center and happened to mention that my husband had just been diagnosed with cancer. As luck, or God, or the stars, would have it, one of the attendees at my workshop came up to me after class and asked what kind of cancer he had. When I told her it was cancer of the small intestine, I could see her jaw drop.

It seems that she received the exact same diagnosis four years earlier. We could hardly believe it. What were the chances of meeting someone in our small town with the same, terribly rare type of cancer? Needless to say, Georgia became our new best friend. She came to our house and shared her success story with us, which was extremely encouraging and just what we needed.

At one point she also had been faced with the same decision. Chemo or no chemo? She chose to go with the chemo and was able to give us her first-hand experience of what the next seven months of our lives would be like. Since she was a journalism major, she had been religious about keeping a written diary of her six months of chemo, day by day, treatment by treatment. She wrote about how she felt, her nausea, what she ate, what she couldn't eat. She described the numbness in her feet, her fatigue and her loss of appetite.

> "... IF THERE IS ONE THING I'VE LEARNED FROM ASTROLOGY IT'S THAT THERE ARE TIMES TO BE CAUTIOUS AND TIMES WHEN "THE STARS" SAY NOW IS THE MOMENT TO STRIKE ..."

This woman was a godsend—and a four-year survivor. She had made it through the terrible chemotherapy which consisted of not only the IV cocktail every three weeks, but chemo pills every day following the IV. This was all too nasty—and a severe shock to the body, but she survived. By now my husband's questions and doubts had all been sufficiently answered, and what to do was becoming crystal clear. He decided to go with it.

He wanted to give himself every chance to beat this horrible disease. Even though he was deemed "clean," it was a very aggressive strain of cancer and there could still be some free radicals floating around in his body. Although the seven months of chemo were not going to be a picnic, he felt it would give him a better chance of beating the odds.

I was in full support of whatever he wanted to do. I knew that our lives were going to change drastically. Maybe this will sound obvious, but there is just never a good time to have cancer. There is no way to prepare for that kind of news. We knew that we would not be able to travel during his seven months of treatment. His energy level would be very low. He could be nauseous. He would not be able to play golf or feel like doing much of anything.

This was going to change our life dramatically. We both loved to travel and frequently played golf together. Yes, our life was going to change. But if there is one thing I've learned from astrology it's that there are times to be cautious and times when "the stars" say now is the moment to strike, to move forward decisively. In such times action is much more likely to bear fruit. As I'll explain later, this was one of those times for me.

I had always wanted to write a book sharing my own path to astrology and my experiences as an astrological counselor, including all the wonderful people whose lives I have touched, and who in turn have brought joy into my life. I had taken several creative writing classes over the years, but nothing really came of it. So when my husband was diagnosed with cancer and I knew that I would have a great deal of time without him, I decided to start writing. This is my journey.

Oh, and by the way, Tony completed his chemo long before the book was completed. He is doing great.

"All the world's a stage,
and all the men and women merely players;
they have their exits and their entrances,
and one man in his time plays many parts."

~ Shakespeare, *As You Like It*

CHAPTER TWO

THE SEARCH FOR MYSELF

DRIFTING, DRIFTING, DRIFTING ...

It was the early 1980s when I made a career move to Stuart, Florida. With no family, no friends, and no emotional support within two hundred miles, I felt like a ship adrift without an anchor. I was totally alone without friends or family close by.

I was looking forward to my new adventure in sales and marketing at this luxurious waterfront resort. It even had a marina where I could dock my sail boat. I was looking forward to my new position, which involved developing a sales and marketing plan to bring group and convention business to the resort.

Although I loved my job, which required long hours,

I continued to feel very alone and isolated when the day came to an end. I guess that is what motivated me to seek outside interests other than work and sailing.

I was fortunate. The local college offered a variety of different and unusual subjects, one of which was astrology. This was long before astrology was as mainstream as it is today. Since I was single and looking for "Mr. Right," I had picked up a couple of "astrological compatibility" books at the bookstores over the years. When I saw the opportunity to actually take a class and learn more about astrology, I was really excited.

I also took classes in Spanish, real-estate and how to fly an airplane—although I must admit that the astrology class was the only one that stuck with me. I never learned to speak Spanish, and I never learned how to fly an airplane. Nor did I pursue a career in real-estate.

What I did learn was fascinating and satisfying, and seemed to answer a lot of questions I had about things I was experiencing in my life. Although I didn't master the Spanish language, I did learn another language, the "Language of Astrology." And what a captivating language it turned out to be. Little did I realize it at the time, but astrology would soon open a whole new world for me—a world in which understanding myself, my family, my co-workers and friends wasn't such a mystery. What I learned, to my initial amazement, was that results here in this world are a direct product of when something is initiated. Timing, it turns out, really is everything.

It would be a mistake to imagine me in those days as some kind of "spiritual seeker" searching for a connection with the universe, or seeking the meaning of life. The truth is that I was just trying to get to know myself better and figure out why I do the things I do, and why I was feeling so

KELLY LOWE

unsure about everything. I didn't want lofty wisdom about the supernatural, eternity, or the spiritual realm. Later on in life I would ask such questions of myself, but at this point I wanted something concrete, and astrology offered concrete explanations.

As a result of this class and my own studies I was eager to seek a professional interpretation of my astrology chart. I inquired about making an appointment for an astrological consultation with my teacher at the college, but she was not seeing new clients at that time. However, she did refer me to a woman who lived in Hollywood, Florida. When I called Brenda to make my first astrology consultation appointment, she asked for my date, time and place of birth.

"SINCE THEN, THE CLOSER I HAVE LOOKED, THE MORE ASTROLOGY HAS MADE SENSE— NOT JUST IN GENERAL, BUT IN ALMOST EVERY INSTANCE IT HAS TESTED POSITIVE ..."

The hour-and-a-half drive from Stuart to Hollywood was filled with anticipation and excitement. What was this stranger going to tell me? Would she be able to help me sort out the dilemmas that I was experiencing in my life? Was she going to recognize that my life was in turmoil? Was she going to see that I was in my season of discontent? Would she see that I wanted to sell everything I owned and take off to sail around the world on my sailboat? That, although I had relocated and made a career change, I was still like a ship without an anchor? I was adrift. I felt that something was about to happen or that a change was coming in my life but I didn't know what, or when it was going to happen.

I was going to see Brenda with so many questions in my mind. I was seeking direction and answers. I wanted to better understand myself and why I was feeling the rest-

9

lessness that troubled me so. But I was also feeling hope-ful. Because the usual answers from the mainstream had failed to give me peace, and because I had already started studying astrology at the college, I went to see Brenda without a bit of skepticism. I was ready to listen, learn, and apply her insightful information. I was eager to learn.

Since then, the closer I have looked, the more astrol-ogy has made sense—not just in general, but in almost ev-ery instance it has tested positive when I compared what it indicated might happen and what actually did happen in my life and the lives of my friends, family and clients. Since that day in Brenda's office, I have understood and appreci-ated myself much more. Of course, I've faced life's usual problems, but I never again felt I had nowhere to turn for answers or explanations.

I still remember as if it were yesterday the moment that I walked into her office. Although I had given her only my birth information—date, time and place—over the phone when I made the appointment, it appeared that she already knew me very well.

Prior to my arrival she had calculated my astrological chart by placing all of the planets in the respective signs and degrees where they had been positioned at the time and place of my birth. She then placed the planets in the respective houses. Of course I didn't realize exactly what all of this meant at the time since I had not yet learned all the nuances of this new language.

From this chart Brenda was able to describe my per-sonality, my likes and dislikes, and my family background. From my astrology chart, which she had prepared before I arrived, she could see that I was the first born in my family and that I had taken on responsibility at an early age. She could see that I was a very responsible person and that I took myself very seriously. She could see that my father had been in the military and I had traveled extensively to foreign countries in my youth. She could see that my love of travel carried over into my adult life, which led me to become a flight attendant and later seek a career in the hotel business which afforded me opportunity to continue my love for traveling the world.

She explained upfront that this astrological consultation was going to be about my past, present and future. I immediately thought, "How exciting is that?" This is going to be all about *me*. She explained that the past is important because astrology is about the study of cycles, and cycles repeat themselves. So by going back to the last time a cycle took place and remembering how we reacted to it or used it, we can benefit from the cycle when it repeats itself.

She then explained that I was currently experiencing one of the most critical and important cycles in my life. As you can imagine, that really got my attention! I knew that there was something really big going on in my life, but I just couldn't put my finger on what it was. Maybe this would explain the discontent and restlessness that I was feeling.

She explained that Saturn, the planet that rules structure, discipline and responsibility was traveling through my 4th house of home and family matters. This meant that I needed to get in touch with my roots, with my innermost personal life. It was an excellent time for psychotherapy or other consciousness raising, consciousness expanding studies. She said it might also bring about a change in residence.

Since the 4th house is the parental axis in the chart, this is also the time when you may have to take on a parental responsibility for someone, or take care of one of your parents. She explained that this would be a tremendous growth cycle for me. A "growth cycle" sounded exciting, but I later learned what that really meant. It meant suck it up and do whatever you need to do, because for the next couple of years life was not going to be a bowl of cherries.

That was news to me. I had been thinking that my next move might be to quit my job and sail around the world on my boat. It was during this time in my life that I read the classic book, *Sailing Alone around the World*. This was a sailing memoir by Joshua Slocum about his single-handed global circumnavigation in 1899. As it turned out, that adventure was not to be in my future.

As for my future? Brenda told me that I had Uranus in my 11th house. Of course I had no conception of what that meant, so she translated into simple English. She explained that it was one of the signatures in a chart of an astrologer. She said that I could easily go on to study and work in the field of astrology. This was an area of talent and strength for me. Now that was exciting information! My hopes resonated with that thought. I *did* feel that I was somehow connected to this cosmic science. The very idea of studying and learning more about this new language was exhilarating. Since I had majored in psychology in college, I was very interested in learning another tool with which to analyze myself and others.

I had come in to see Brenda with a lot of ideas in my head about who I was and where I was headed, but none of them felt like the true *me*, none of them fully satisfied me. Now I felt closer to having a true direction. I could feel a new kind of warmth inside, but at the same time I remembered Brenda's words. What would "a growth cycle" turn out to mean?

*"Be at peace and see a clear pattern and plan
running through all your lives.
Nothing is by chance."*

~ Eileen Caddy, **Footprints on the Path**

CHAPTER THREE

THE ADVENTURE BEGINS

RUNNING WITH THE WIND

My father was still a fairly young man and had always appeared to be in good health. In fact he was still working and leading an active and busy life. So you can imagine my shock and dismay when I received an emergency phone call from my mother while I was on a sales trip to Denver, Colorado. My father had suffered a heart attack. At that moment if someone had asked me for my name, I couldn't have answered them, but I did remember very clearly what Brenda had told me during our appointment: "I was about to take on a parental role."

My life was certainly going to change, that much I understood, but to what extent I still could not imagine. What would happen to my aspirations of quitting my job and sailing around the world? I didn't really have time to stop and mourn the end of that dream. My father's life and well-being instantly became my main priorities. Fortunately, the heart attack was not fatal, but he was going to require a great deal of home care before he would be strong enough to endure a heart bypass.

Since my mother was still working and I had been feeling very dissatisfied with my current life, it seemed only logical that I would be the family member to move back home and take care of my father. There was something about this scenario that really appealed to me. I knew in my heart that I was doing what I needed and wanted to do. The consultation with Brenda had given me the insight into my personality and the understanding of the cycle of life

> "WITH ASTROLOGY I COULD SEE HOW SPECIFIC CONNECTIONS ACROSS TIME AND SPACE AFFECT EVENTS IN DAILY LIFE—PAST, PRESENT, AND FUTURE."

that I was in, so that I could happily embrace the task at hand and the opportunity to spend that quality time with my father.

After my life-changing appointment with Brenda in Hollywood, I really became enthralled with this new language and new world that I had discovered. I knew there was truly some connection to the planets for us living on the earth. I could feel cosmic connection in my bones. To say my interest had been sparked would be a complete understatement. In that moment I realized that although my eyesight was 20/20, I had been blindly sleep-walking through life. Now I was beginning to wake up—and to look up. The word "Buddha" means one who is fully awake, and Jesus said spiritual connection requires a mystic rebirth "from above." I never once thought of myself as a prophet or teacher like the Buddha or Jesus, but in that moment I understood that there are infinite possibilities to life that I was just beginning to comprehend. I felt compelled to learn more about this mysterious, intriguing cosmic science called astrology.

So, even after moving away from Stuart, Florida, where I had completed my introduction to astrology class, I continued to expand my studies and seek knowledge whenever and wherever I could.

It was during this cycle in my life, that I took a Transcendental Meditation (TM) class and began the practice of daily meditation. I was introduced to the work of Edgar Cayce, one of the most prolific psychics in the twentieth century. I studied Tarot Cards, dream analysis, and numerology in addition to continuing my astrology studies.

And then came an exciting breakthrough. I met a woman named Betty Riley who helped change my life. She was a psychic medium who had written a book called *A Vale Too Thin—Out of Control*. Her true experience of reincarnation is one of the best documented cases on record. Without going too deeply into Betty Riley's story, she was a psychic of remarkable ability whose awareness of her past lives manifested in her present life. Her ability to see things far beyond the limitations of most people was so powerfully real that university researchers sought to find a viable explanation. So, when Betty saw something in me that I had not seen in myself, and encouraged me to pursue my astrological gifts, I knew that my path had been chosen. And, as I envisioned taking my life's work to a higher level, I also understood that the thing which made it a *higher* level was the opportunity for helping and working with others.

It was through my metaphysical studies, Betty's

encouragement, and the seed that Brenda had planted during that first appointment that my interest and passion for astrology grew. After years of studying and observing the movement of the planets as they affect me and the lives of my family and friends, my avocation eventually was to become my vocation. My focus had moved beyond the search for myself; I had been given a gift and I knew it was meant to be shared.

As an astrology counselor, I feel that I am standing on solid ground. People throughout history have looked to the "heavens" as a way of explaining why things happen as they do, but so often the best they can come up with is, "It must have been God's will." Those can be comforting words but they don't really say much, and are usually uttered after the fact. That has never been enough for me. With astrology I could see how specific connections across time and space affect events in daily life—in the past, present, and future.

So I began my journey in earnest. I bought what seemed like a truckload of astrology books and continued with my studies. This was before the internet. I attended astrology conferences and conventions whenever I could. I studied with a mentor for several years and took a series of classes whenever and wherever I could.

*"We learn wisdom from failure much more than
from success; we often discover what will do by finding
out what will not do; and probably he who
never made a mistake never made a discovery."*
~ Samuel Smiles

CHAPTER FOUR

THE NEXT STEP OF THE JOURNEY

THE BASICS ... AND BEYOND

There are a few basics that make the language of astrology easier to understand. One basic, as I will show later, is that the forces described by astrology are at work whether or not you are aware of them. But on an even more fundamental level, my studies revealed to me that despite all its complexities, a basic definition of astrology can be simply stated: Astrology is the study of repeating cycles. These cycles can be understood through the study of the movement of the planets and how they affect us as they move at their varied speeds and distances in ever-changing aspect to each other.

The observation of the movement of the planets and

how they influence us goes back thousands of years to the Chaldeans in ancient Babylon. In some traditions the three "wise men" described in the Gospel of Matthew, who came "from the east" to visit Jesus after his birth, are called the "three astrologers." No one knows for sure which region of the east they came from. It could have been Chaldea, or it could have been Persia. But the earliest traditions called them "magi" and we do know that as part of their religion, these magi priests paid particular attention to the stars, and gained an international reputation for astrology, which at that time was already a highly regarded science.

"THE DEEPER I WENT, THE MORE I REALIZED HOW MUCH DEEPER I STILL HAD TO GO ..."

I also learned that astrology is a very comprehensive and accurate tool for comparing individual personalities. It can be used to benefit business endeavors or romantic relationships. It is remarkably accurate for analyzing compatibility. Since I was single at the time, the more I learned about compatibility the more I wanted to learn. The more I observed and experienced astrology in action, the more I learned about the intricacies of how it worked, and how dramatically it could influence a person's life. It remains true today that the majority of people who come to my workshops come because they want to learn about themselves and their prospects for romance and relationship.

Astrology was without a doubt the most amazing tool for self evaluation that I had ever discovered. Since I had majored in psychology, I was always interested in personal analysis. But there was more to it. I learned that astrology is not only a way to analyze personalities; it is also a way to plan activities and schedule events in order to achieve the most desirable outcome.

The deeper I went, the more I realized how much deeper I still had to go—depths that couldn't even be imagined from the surface. This was not a game or a pastime; this was serious; it was about people's lives. That realization gave me a feeling inside that is hard to describe.

I also learned that the revelations of astrology are conveyed in a very specific and complex language, and learning this exciting new language would require a great deal of studying and memorizing. Studying "Sun sign compatibility" while I was in search of Mr. Right was a convenient introduction to astrology for me. It motivated me and made it fun, but I was well aware that there was a lot more below the surface that I was going to have to delve into before I could truly appreciate this new language.

I learned that an astrology chart is a picture of the sky at the moment when a person is born. This is what the saying, "as above, so below" refers to. I learned that a person's astrology chart was like the stage setting for a play and that the planets are the characters. The Sun plays the leading role—the character at center stage—and all of the other planets are the supporting actors. The Moon plays the role of the emotions, while Venus plays cupid. Mars plays the role of the energizer bunny, while Mercury plays the scholar and intellectual role. Jupiter plays the eternal optimist and traveler. Saturn is the disciplinarian and teacher.

Neptune, Uranus and Pluto often speak from backstage, and being more distant from the leading character, the Sun, it is not always as obvious what their role is. But if you pay close attention you will see that Neptune plays the dreamer, and Pluto's role is the transformer and controller. Uranus is pretty unpredictable, so we never know exactly what he is going to do. We just know that we should expect the unexpected when he makes his entrance.

As I said, astrology, like every other field of arts and science, has its fundamentals that must be mastered. They often are a challenge that many can't get past. I first had to memorize all of the symbols for the Sun signs and planets. I learned that in Western astrology the astrological chart is divided into twelve houses and each house represents an area of your life. Each house has a planet that rules it. And each house represents a different area of your life and different part of your body. For example, the 2nd house describes your finances and the way you perceive money. It also rules your throat. The 6th house describes you health and how you take care of yourself (*to review the 12 houses, revisit* **Words to Guide You ...** *page X*).

I learned that a person's Sun sign does not work alone in describing their personality. It is also important to know in what sign their Moon, Venus, Mars and all of the other planets were located in their chart. Like all other studies, astrology has basic resource books that help unravel mysteries. I learned how to use a book called *The American Ephemeris for the 20th Century*. Now there is an *American Ephermeris for the 21st Century*. It is the calculation of the position of the planets going back through the centuries and going forward.

MY QUEST FOR KNOWLEDGE

The more I learned the stronger I felt, and the more I wanted to learn. I was gaining tools and skills, and wisdom. I felt more ... able. I liked feeling strong and able, and I wanted even more of it. But the more I studied, the more I realized my journey had only just begun. One of my first astrology text books was *Astrology, a Cosmic Science* by the late Isabel M. Hickey. From this well-organized and in-depth book, I memorized and learned the basics about astrology. I felt like I was overflowing with details of this fascinating cosmic study called astrology, but little did I know that I was still just starting out on what was to be a long and very personal journey with my newfound language.

I became a regular attendee at the United Astrology Congresses (also known as UAC), and studied with the best astrologers in the field. My goal was to develop my skills and knowledge to their highest capacity so I could see my own motivations more clearly, and to help others reap the benefits that I was beginning to enjoy. The UAC conferences provided a fast track to my goal. One of my favorites was in spectacular Monterey, California, where a multitude of famous, knowledgeable and experienced astrological authors and speakers shared their insights. The late Marion March, who helped found the UAC and co-authored the highly inspirational book, *The Only Way to Learn Astrology*, presented a workshop titled "In-depth Horoscope Analysis." Little did I know that when I was enjoying the magnificent view of Monterey Bay I was gazing at the place where my favorite singer, John Denver, would one day suffer his fatal airplane accident.

The UAC conferences always offer a good mix of generalists like Ms. March, and specialists like financial astrologer Arch Crawford. Arch had been a regular guest on CNBC, *20/20*, *Nightly Business Report* and *Good Morning America*. He was ranked among the top market timers in the popular rating services, and designated as "The Street's best known Astrologer," according to Barron's. Also featured was Georgia Stathis, internationally known speaker and author of *Business Astrology 101*, who shared her experience and knowledge of how astrology can be used in the business world. Since her business background was in real estate, she was able to share a great deal of practical knowledge and experience in her workshop.

It is well known that many people look to astrology for guidance on enhancing their lives and personal relationships, especially their love relationships. But in addition many also seek guidance in subjects like improving their business or money making skills. At one particular conference, business and finance was the theme of all the workshops that I attended.

I had the pleasure at another UAC conference of hearing Michael Luten, a very popular and entertaining New York astrologer and columnist for *Vanity Fair* magazine, who wrote the book *Childhood Rising*.

Among the elite inspirational speakers was psychotherapist and former Catholic monk, Thomas Moore, who had always been one of my favorite authors. I had read all of his books: *Care of the Soul*, *The Planets Within*, *The Soul of Sex*, *The Re-Enchantment of Everyday Life*, and *Original Self*. Because I had also come from a Catholic background I totally identified and connected with his work. When I saw that he was going to be our keynote speaker at the UAC convention I was ecstatic. I could hardly believe that I was really going to hear Thomas Moore speak. And I must say I was not disappointed.

I don't mention these names because they are celebrities. What impressed me so much was their depth of understanding, and how serious they were about astrology. I absorbed mounds of information from them and started to fully understand the importance of what I was doing. And I saw that the best people in the field were grounded in the basic principles.

Because the main principle of astrology is "as above, so below," the basics are "in the stars" and not dependent on any individual astrologer's practice. But what was becoming clearer and clearer to me is that although anyone can be taught to see the primary details of an astrology chart, the real art of astrology is in helping clients understand how the information can impact their lives. After all, the planets point us in a certain direction but it's up to us to decide whether we want to swim with the current, or against it.

Since the best teachers are usually also the best students, no one—even the acclaimed astrologers I've mentioned—is beyond learning more. Humility served me well. I wanted to soak up every bit of knowledge I could, and I didn't mind one bit sitting at the feet of the masters. Each time I listened to a different speaker, I felt I was being handed a new piece of the puzzle. As I assembled it piece by piece I began to see the whole picture more clearly, which made me all the more eager to press on and acquire the missing pieces.

At the Atlanta UAC I was totally blown away by the famous speaker and author, Noel Tyl. I actually treated myself to an appointment with him. That was another very insightful session. I was certainly not in the same place or dealing with the same issues when I attended this conference as when I met with Brenda, but I wanted to have another consultation to help me plan and deal with the cycles that were currently affecting my chart.

Since your natal astrology chart is continually affected by the transits, or movement of the planets, it continues to supply us with additional information—information that is very helpful in planning and preparing for the future. It is a living process—life in motion.

It just so happens that I was experiencing another critical "Saturn cycle" when I met with Noel. It takes Saturn

29 years to travel completely around a chart, with every seven years being critical and significant times in a person's life. It just so happened that my appointment with Noel was 14 years after my first appointment with Brenda in Hollywood, Florida. Only this time, I was preparing to get married and change residence. As I would discover in my own practice, people do tend to seek counseling when they are going through tough times or changes in their life. We all seem to sail very nicely through the easy, enjoyable cycles, but watch out when a crisis comes along. That's when astrology can help us understand how to deal with it, and tell us how long it will last.

Noel Tyl has many books to his credit; my favorite is *Prediction in Astrology*. I would not recommend this for beginners, but it's a great book for a serious student of astrology to have in their library.

As my quest for knowledge grew, I attended UAC conferences in Washington, D.C., and Chicago. I was even fortunate to have a UAC conference come to Orlando, which was my home town at that time. I was continually learning and absorbing knowledge from the teachers—the professionals and experts in the language of astrology.

Because I love to travel it doesn't take much of an excuse for me to pack a suitcase. So there I was at a special conference in Greece on the Isle of Kos where I studied ancient and medical astrology. I was like a sponge with an endless thirst for knowledge. The more I absorbed, the more I wanted.

Although Dayton, Ohio, was not nearly as exciting as Greece, I did attend a small conference there, where I was first introduced to the late Sophia Mason's work. I found her to be an amazing teacher and person. Her books are small, but very succinct and powerful. My favorites are

You and Your Ascendant, and *Forecasting with New, Full & Quarter Moons through The Houses*. Sophia's work can be appreciated by both the novice and the professional astrologer.

Some people like to think of breakthroughs as happening in an instant. Like driving around lost and suddenly spotting the address you've been searching for—an epiphany, a light suddenly turning on in the darkness, a chance to shout "eureka, I've found it!" My "breakthrough" came years earlier when I realized astrology would be the path that led me to a better understanding of myself. From there I walked the path for many years, growing in knowledge and wisdom before the path opened up on a beautiful clearing and I knew I had arrived. My life changed and I knew I had been given a precious gift I could share with others. Everything I had been through was now worthwhile. I could smile and say to myself, "yes, I see."

*"For those who believe, no proof is necessary.
For those who don't believe, no proof is possible."*
~ John and Lyn St. Clair Thomas, **Eyes of the Beholder**

CHAPTER FIVE

THE CLEAR LIGHT OF THE SUN

LEARNING TO TRUST MY SENSES

As I studied, as I observed life in action, I was convinced that we are without a doubt affected by the "rotation of the planets." The movements of the Sun and Moon provide the most obvious correlations for human behavior since the naked eye can witness everything as it relates to events that are taking place in our lives. Using the Sun and Moon as examples, we can easily grasp how the movement of the planets affects us. This doesn't require advanced study in astrology.

The easiest observation is the cycle of the seasons. During the winter season when the daylight hours are shorter our productivity level seems to decline. In the summer when the daylight hours are longer we seem to have a boundless supply of energy.

ALASKA IN AUGUST

A perfect example of this can be seen in the extreme northern latitudes. I recall flying into Anchorage, Alaska, (the land of the midnight Sun) with the glow of the golden Sun still there over the mountains at twelve midnight.

Although I had been traveling for many hours, my body was fooled into thinking that I was ready to start a new day. The Sun appeared to be rising, which created the feeling of a new dawn. Eventually of course, we all must sleep, but our sleep patterns certainly seem to be affected by the rotation of the Sun's light.

As I traveled through Alaska during the entire month of August I was amazed to actually feel what it was like to live in an environment where the Sun never sets. There just never seemed to be a good time to go to bed. I had to have blackout curtains on the windows in order to be able to sleep. The stores were open all of the time. People were shopping in the middle of the night. I thought it was crazy.

Even children respond to the rotation of the Sun. When my son was very young he visited one summer with his father, who was living in Scotland at the time. His main complaint was that he had to go to bed when the Sun was still up.

The Sun is just one easily recognized example of how the relative positions of the planets affect us as we journey through life on earth. Of course, just as the Sun is at the center of an astrological chart, it has throughout history been a center point for so many visions which try to explain the way things are. That's not surprising, since without the Sun there would be no life. Spiritual thinkers of many types have looked to the heavens for understanding of why things turn out the way they do. Sometimes the answers are simple. No one would dispute that our attitude begins to shift as the days stretch out in the spring and the Sun moves closer to us in the northern hemisphere. The Sun's rays reach us on a more direct path and we feel its power more fully. Is it any surprise that in this time of increased energy from the Sun *we* also feel increased energy?

We do "spring cleaning" in the spring for a reason. The Sun's energy makes spring the time to take on big jobs. And since we all accept that the position of the Sun in relation to the earth influences our behavior, does it take a quantum leap of faith to believe that the position of the planets in our solar system also affect our lives here on earth? The experiences of my own life— and the lives of my friends, family and clients—tend to demonstrate that the rotation of the planets has a definite affect on what happens in our day-to-day existence.

> "FORTUNATELY, FOR THOSE WHO LIKE TO KEEP THEIR REALITY GROUNDED IN PREDICTABLE OUTCOMES, ASTROLOGY HAS BEEN DOING JUST THAT FOR THOUSANDS OF YEARS."

RAINY DAYS — THERE AIN'T NO SUNSHINE

The absence of the Sun on cloudy or rainy days also teaches a lesson. On those rainy days when the Sun fails to appear, you might want to just turn over in bed, pull the covers up and go back to sleep. But they also are wonderful for reading and enjoying a little "down time." A little rain can be rejuvenating. It gives us a chance to pause for a moment in our busy lives, clear out the cobwebs in our brain and catch up on our rest, but too much rain can be depressing and unproductive. Most of us can make it through one or two dark, rainy days without much effect on the mind, but anyone who ever claimed that the heavens don't affect us certainly didn't live in an area where it can rain for days and days.

As humans, we sometimes tend to over-complicate things and deny the simple truth we see with our own eyes. Wisdom can come to us from many sources. It doesn't have to come from a laboratory at Harvard or M.I.T. It is often handed down through the ages and verified through life experience. This is how the truths of astrology have come to us.

Many thoughtful people these days accept that discernment can come from a variety of sources. And more and more, our awareness bubbles up all over the landscape. The wisdom of "times gone by" is honored alongside the discoveries of esteemed scientists. So much of what we learned from nature over time has been forgotten—or dismissed as folklore even though results were carefully observed and shared with others. The sages and seers of ancient cultures—like the midwives and healers whom the Puritans of New England called witches—possessed a knowledge with deep roots reaching back through time and space. They lived closer to nature than our mechanized way of life today allows.

Unfortunately, most of us have been taught to doubt anything that can't be proved with a Bunsen burner and a test tube. Faith and intuitive knowledge have been scorned as superstition, even though in many ways they are based on observations of the environment and human behavior. Fortunately, for those who like to keep their reality grounded in predictable facts and outcomes, astrology has been doing just that for thousands of years.

Still, there are those who like to control what is and isn't "believable." But the truth always resurfaces somehow—in books or movies, on the internet, or in the lyrics of our music. When it comes to how a lack of sunshine influences us, Karen Carpenter's "Rainy Days and Mondays Always Get Me Down" says it very nicely. Then there's the song "Ain't No Sunshine When She's Gone." Both songs express what we know firsthand as people experiencing life—that sunshine makes us happy and rainy days do not.

Both songs also express an obvious fact which so many of us resist as we strive to be complete masters of our own destiny: Factors and forces outside of ourselves profoundly affect our personal reality. The good news from astrology is that these forces are not random. In fact, they are predictable and measurable. They come and go like clockwork as the Moon repeats it cycles, and the earth and the planets rotate and revolve around the Sun in a pattern which seems as eternal as time itself.

So, the first step toward accepting how astrology can help guide our lives is to simply look around us and observe. Few would dispute that when the Sun is dominating the sky our mood is more likely to be optimistic. A dark and cloudy sky—if it goes on too long—has the opposite effect. If you have ever rented a place at the beach for a week with a couple of small children and it rained, you know just what I'm talking about.

I will speak in more depth later about how the Moon affects us, but the impact of a Full Moon is one more way in which the effects of the planets can be clearly correlated and verified. It is well known that the Full Moon's influence is felt in the fluids of our bodies and can be measured by increases in crime and other crazy behavior. So, when we judge by our experiences, it becomes obvious that we are affected by the rotation of the planets. We are able to see the Sun and the Moon more clearly, but all of the planets have an impact on our daily lives. And since the planets move in a systematic rotation and repeat the rotation, we can learn from our history.

*"Man cannot discover new oceans
until he has courage to lose sight of the shore."*

~ Unknown Author

CHAPTER SIX

FROM STUDENT TO TEACHER

HOIST THE MAIN SAIL

I was very blessed to have had the opportunity to study under and learn from some very exceptional and gifted astrologers during my early, formative years. I have always had a strong attraction to the old Nissan commercial, "life's a journey, enjoy the ride." As I began to study and learn astrology I gained a much better understanding of myself and those around me, and I started enjoying the ride through life much more. I began to realize that astrology helps illuminate the major scheme of life, which can help us understand and enjoy life more fully.

Opportunity for experience can present itself in many forms. I can recall sitting in a lecture many years ago listening to Carol Rushman, an astrological teacher whom I greatly admire. She told personal stories about how her very large family had provided ample opportunity for learning and watching astrology in action. This gave her lots of first-hand experience as she watched her children growing up. Seeing and observing the movement of the planets as they affect a person's life on an ongoing basis is an invaluable resource.

Although I did not have a large family, I did have the good fortune to be the resident astrologer at a dude ranch for many years, which offered women's get-away weekends. I found this to be extremely interesting, and accelerating to my development. On the weekends that I spent at the ranch, I had the opportunity to study and work with hundreds of women's astrology charts. This gave me what was the equivalent of years and years of astrological counseling experience in a very compact and concentrated period of time.

"LEARNING THIS NEW LANGUAGE WAS TURNING OUT TO BE A LOT OF FUN AND I WAS LIKE A KID WITH A BOX OF CHOCOLATE."

While I was working in the hotel business, my job required a great deal of travel, calling on potential businesses and working trade shows. In those days traveling was fun and exciting. Setting up and tearing down booths at conventions and conferences, smiling and greeting a stream of potential customers seemed more like play than work. I got to stay in some very nice five-star hotels like the Plaza in New York, and saw some wonderful Broadway shows. It was a whirlwind existence, and at the time I never questioned how long it would continue. When I look back I know there was a certain amount of stress to it, but at the time it felt like life was giving me everything I wanted. Those earlier moments I'd spent feeling confused about myself—who I am and where I was headed— were washed away by the excitement I was feeling, and by learning this new language and applying it to my life.

So, for a while, my old life continued even as my new life was being born. It was hectic but fun. I'll never forget the beautiful train trip across Canada that I enjoyed while doing a Disney promotion with Eastern Airlines. At that time I was working in sales for a hotel at Disney and we were visiting the Eastern Airlines Reservations Centers and doing sales promotions in the evening. I have so many fond memories of those days.

Working at the Travel Trade Show in London, England, was also very exciting. This was all a lot fun when I was young and energetic, but it was also exhausting. There was always a lot of work to catch up on when I returned to the office. Eventually I began to wonder how long it could go on. I could not see myself living that hectic lifestyle as a senior citizen.

Anyone who has ever shared that kind of lifestyle will know what I mean. The exhilaration is incredible, but spending endless hours on your feet wearing a constant happy face begins to take its toll. I woke up one day asking myself the ultimate question: how long am I going to continue doing this? Needing answers, I turned again to astrology and an unexpected peace began to envelop me. I felt that revealing the insights of astrology to others was something that I could continue to enjoy doing until I left this planet. They say that experience is the great teacher and I believe it's true. My sales and marketing work had propelled me at breakneck speed through time and space, and when I stopped long enough to think about it, I realized that all these experiences would be a positive factor in understanding how the planets affect our lives. I was completing my time of preparation. The more life cycles that I observed and lived through, the more I learned, and the better equipped I became to eventually share my knowledge with my clients and friends.

I don't recall making an actual decision to move from hotel sales and marketing to astrological counselor. I think my friend Betty was probably one of the major influences. Her words kept ringing in my ear: "You have a gift." And I kept thinking about the seed that Brenda had planted during my first appointment with her: "You have the signature of an astrologer in your chart." As the stars would have it, all the pieces began falling into place.

Although I had learned how to mathematically calculate an astrology chart by hand, it was the computer age that really got me jump-started as an astrologer. Once I got a computer software program that would calculate the charts, the sky was literally the limit for me. I will always be eternally grateful for the home computer. The computer enabled me to study my friends and families' charts. I even studied the charts of the men that I dated and used those calculations to decide whether I would continue to date them. Learning this new language was turning out to be a lot of fun and I was like a kid with a box of chocolate.

There's an old song that says "you don't know what you've got until you lose it." The opposite is also true—you don't know what you need until you find it. Just when I needed an inspirational friend and colleague to encourage me, I found Betty through the Spiritual Advisory Council. Betty was the Medium I mentioned earlier who had written a book about her life experience. I was fascinated not only by her book but by the fact we shared the same birthday. I recall making a joke about it and telling her that Elton John also shared our birthday. Now that has to count for something . . .

As it turned out, Betty became my friend and inspiration. It was through her encouragement that I eventually decided to take the leap and make the transition from astrology as an avocation to my vocation.

PART II

SHARING MY JOURNEY ...
AND MAKING THE MOST OF LIFE

"A JOURNEY IS LIKE MARRIAGE.
THE CERTAIN WAY TO BE WRONG
IS TO THINK YOU CONTROL IT."

JOHN STEINBECK

"Be realistic: Plan for a miracle."

~ Bhagwan Shree Rajneesh

CHAPTER SEVEN

EXPANSION, OPTIMISM AND DISCIPLINE

FROM JUPITER TO SATURN

Experiencing life is like riding a wave on the ocean. It's like watching the Sun rise and set. You might be busy preparing for a storm or enjoying a warm sunny day on the beach. Or it can be like preparing for a sunny day and getting a storm instead. Despite all of the elements which seem repetitious or familiar, life is constantly presenting us with something new. We are constantly building, preparing and repairing our lives. With the help of astrology we can do it better. It can be less painful, more gratifying and more predictable. Life truly is a journey, and through the use of astrology you can enjoy the ride more comfortably.

There will always be ups and downs, bumps in the road, good days and bad days, but understanding and working with your astrology chart can certainly prepare you for all of life's trials and tribulations.

Astrology can help you take advantage of the positive, advantageous good cycles that are coming up and it can help you prepare for and work through the difficult, more challenging cycles.

You could say that life accumulates as we live through these cycles. Hopefully we learn from them and discover how to take better advantage of the best and worst of times. It has been my desire for many years to compile my personal and professional experiences—the lessons learned through trials and tribulations which have guided me and my clients through this journey called life. In one sense, astrology is an experience of seeing ourselves in a larger context, of stepping far enough back from all the details which tend to cloud the big picture. Remembering that our natal chart is a picture of the sky at our moment of birth, there's great comfort in knowing there is an order to the universe that can be identified and understood, and that life is not just a series of random and disconnected moments. If we don't fight against these influences, if we let the universe have its way, things will generally turn out as they should and we will live a more fulfilled and stress free life.

Since this is a journey through my experiences, and since it always feels better to begin with the positive and pleasant experiences, that is exactly what I am going to do.

I can recall many years ago thinking about wanting to write a book. So I enrolled in a creative writing class at Rollins College. It was my heart's desire to share my experiences as they related to life's journey and the connection there is with astrology. But I guess I had not acquired enough of life's experience, nor was I ready to undertake what seemed to be too daunting a task. But now the saying "all things in their own time" has been proven valid once again, and my time for laying out the wisdom of my lessons learned is finally imminent.

THE JUPITER CONNECTION

One of the most enjoyable cycles that a person can experience is the cycle of Jupiter connecting with their Sun. This takes place approximately every 12 years. Unless there is some other overwhelmingly difficult cycle that is taking place at the same time, this can be one of the best times in a person's life.

After many years of being single and kissing a lot of frogs, I finally met my *Prince Charming* when transiting Jupiter was approaching my natal Sun. Since I was a student of astrology at the time, I appreciated the timing and significance of this relationship.

I had learned from my astrology studies—and experienced in my personal life—that this was considered one of the most benefic and enjoyable transits. To clarify in English, the word transit simple refers to the movement of a traveling planet across the sky. I knew that this was to be the beginning of a marvelous cycle. It was a wonderful time to initiate something new and expand my horizons. And it was a great time to broaden my perspective.

And that is exactly what I did. When transiting Jupiter was exactly at the same degree as my natal Sun, Larry and I were married.

In 2005 when Jupiter was traveling though my 3rd house of communications and writing I was inspired and motivated (the influence of Jupiter) to begin writing a book. Although the timing was right astrologically and my intentions and desire were there at the time, other priorities took precedence and the book was put on the back burner. Perhaps I had still not acquired enough experience and discipline to continue the task at that time.

At the writing of this book, Jupiter was traveling through my 9th house which rules teaching, publication and inspiration. I was definitely motivated and inspired. My motivation and inspiration were reinforced by the fact that my natal Sun in my 9th house was being transited by Jupiter. In simple English this means that Jupiter was traveling at the same degree as my natal Sun. This added a strong support to the mission at hand.

Although I would not say that astrology *predicts* the future, it can predict a favorable—or unfavorable—climate for the timing of success. Life is so much better when we can plan to do things at the most beneficial time, which correlates to the astrological cycles in our lives. Since I have always been a swimmer, I like to compare this to swimming downstream rather then swimming upstream. Sailing is another good analogy of the benefits of astrology. A responsible sailor wouldn't think of setting sail without checking the weather first. I can recall only too well the importance of checking the tide tables before trying to sail or motor sail under a bridge. Several years ago, while living in South Florida, I almost ran my sailboat into a bridge as I was trying to motor sail under the bridge against the tide. It's always good to know which way the tide is flowing when you are making your plans in life.

JUPITER AND INSPIRATIONAL CONNECTIONS — YOUR GUARDIAN ANGLES

Strike while the iron is hot. Jupiter, the planet of abundance can be inspiring and motivating ... and if someone comes along with their Sun in the same sign as your Jupiter, it can be magical for you both. You don't know why; you just connect with each other. Often times this person will play an inspirational or motivational role in your life, and you will do the same in theirs as well. These are people who will often promote you, or help you accomplish your dreams and goals. We can't really seek them out, or run an ad on the internet for them. They just seem to come into your life exactly when you need them. They recharge your battery, uplift your spirits and motivate you. I like to call them guardian angels.

> "LIFE IS SO MUCH BETTER WHEN WE CAN PLAN TO DO THINGS AT THE MOST BENEFICIAL TIME, WHICH CORRELATES TO THE ASTROLOGICAL CYCLES IN OUR LIVES."

I am blessed with many guardian angles in my life, some of whom I have become more aware of than others. As an astrologer, I am more inclined than most people to ask a new acquaintance for their birth date when I start associating with them—especially if we are going to develop any kind of a business relationship. But sometimes these angels just show up unanticipated in a social setting and before you know it they have become instrumental in inspiring and promoting you. When you find out later that you have a strong connection, such as a Jupiter/Sun connection, it really doesn't come as a surprise.

Guardian angels can arrive when you least expect them. Joann came to me out of the blue at a golf event. We were attending a social networking breakfast with the Executive Women's Golf Association, where she had a display table for her cosmetic business. I happened to be interested in her product and she was interested in astrology. As our friendship developed she invited me to join NCW, a professional women's networking group that she was a member of. Since I was new to the area and had not met many people, I really did not have a good connection to the business community. So, excited to meet new people and expand my horizons, I joined Networking Connects Women, without any expectations as to where it would take me.

As luck would have it, this group of women turned out to be a wonderful source of networking—much more so than I could ever have hoped for. It was comfortable and easy to develop personal and business relationships with the women. There were many professional services and businesses represented among them, from a wonderful jeweler to an excellent massage therapist whose services I was delighted to avail myself of.

One of the members, Christine, who was the publisher of a local magazine, suggested that I start doing monthly astrology lectures at a local restaurant. She had a contact at a restaurant in town that was interested in sponsoring the event. We decided to call it "Dinner with the Stars."

This was the first time I had done anything publicly since moving to my new home town. As it turned out, this became a springboard which opened a whole new avenue for me. I had the opportunity to introduce astrology to people I otherwise might never have met. My Jupiter/Sun connection with my guardian angel Joann continues to be an inspirational connection and friendship.

Another guardian angel, Krista, was a member of the professional women's networking group. She owns and operates the Daytona Yoga & Wellness Center. Since I have always been drawn to yoga, I was immediately attracted to her. We quickly became friends and kindred spirits. When she invited me to do astrology workshops at her studio, I was delighted. Here again, this opportunity opened the way for me to meet many like-minded, beautiful souls. My Jupiter/Sun connection with Krista also continues to be an inspirational connection and friendship.

One day, while I was in the midst of getting started with writing this book, I was surprised by an unsolicited email from guardian angel Krista. She forwarded me a notice she had received about a workshop titled, "Independent Book Publishing—Six Steps to Success." I immediately rearranged my schedule so that I could attend the workshop, which happened to be taking place the very next day. The timing was perfect. It was exactly what I was looking for and I was not disappointed.

When I arrived at the studio on the day of the workshop, I immediately noticed a tall, striking gentleman standing toward the front of the room with whom I felt an instant connection. I was not surprised to learn that he was conducting the workshop. As the class began I couldn't help wondering what his Sun sign might be, or what connection we might have in our astrological charts. So at the conclusion of the workshop I asked him about his birthday. Since I had identified myself as an astrologer during the introductions, I felt that it gave me the liberty to be so bold to ask him. He didn't seem to object, although he did whisper the year in my ear. I immediately recognized that his Sun sign was conjunct by Jupiter which I shared with him.

His puzzled and bewildered look again reminded me that astrology is a language onto itself and most people do not speak it. So, using simple non-astrological English, I quickly tried to explain that we shared an astrological connection, in that his Sun sign was in the same sign as my Jupiter. This was a very interesting and positive connection. Since I was on a time crunch to leave and there were other people from the class waiting to speak with him, I tried to make the explanation as concise as possible. I took his card and casually said I would look at his chart as I was interested in how we might hit it off working together. I would get back with him to perhaps ask him to help me with my book. But at that point I already knew that I had met another guardian angel. I knew that he was going be instrumental in editing and helping me publish my book.

Guarding angels do seem to arrive when you least expect them and exactly when you need them most. It has happened to me so often that I really have started expecting them to be there for me. Wouldn't it be interesting if everyone had their astrological Sun sign and the sign their Jupiter was in at the time they were born displayed on their forehead? This would enable everyone to instantly identify their guardian angels and they could identify you. However, I do believe that we are intuitively attracted to those people who are inspirational and helpful to us. They often remain in our lives indefinitely.

GIRLFRIENDS FOREVER

Some people pass through your life like a ship in the night, while others remain as pillars of stability and friendship that can last a life time.

Such was the case of two dynamic, special women who have been supportive and lasting friends in my life for many years. I have always believed that there are no such thing as coincidence. I believe that we meet everyone at the right time, in the right place and just when we are supposed to meet them.

When Jupiter, the planet of optimism and expansion, was traveling through my 11th house I decided to join our local Toastmasters organization. The 11th house deals with groups, clubs and organizations, and with getting in touch with your hopes, goals, dreams and wishes. I had always wanted to be a public speaker. Since I knew that timing was everything, I chose this particular cycle to develop my speaking skills and my confidence. I wanted to become more socially interactive and share my experiences with astrology in a more public forum. It was my intention to eventually speak about astrology in a light and entertaining way at conventions and organizations. I knew this would be an excellent time to take on this study.

As it turned out, it wasn't very long before I was speaking at conventions, clubs, groups and organizations throughout the state.

Once you begin experiencing how the movement of the planets influences us, you no longer hope for the desired outcome, you simply expect it and gain confidence in what you are doing. So I sailed on, feeling assurance that this would be a productive time for me to take the understanding of life I had gained from astrology out into the larger world.

As I worked through the Toastmasters manual, diligently learning how to prepare my speeches, I was befriended by Liz, who was to become my mentor. It just so happened that Liz and I had a Sun/Jupiter connection. Her Sun was at the same degree and sign as my Jupiter. As I mentioned before, this usually proves to be a very uncomplicated, enjoyable, beneficial and long lasting friendship.

As luck or "the stars" would have it, Liz not only mentored me though my Toastmasters speeches, she also introduced me to an entirely new circle of woman friends. She was a member of Beta Sigma Phi, a women's professional sorority which happened to be pledging new members.

This is where I met Rita, a long-time dear friend of Liz's. Notice I don't say "old friend." She would never forgive me. I wasn't surprised to learn that Rita's Moon was in the same degree and sign as my Jupiter. This is also an indication of an endearing, long-lasting friendship. So Liz, Rita and I enjoyed the bond of a strong Jupiter/Sun/Moon connection. It is no surprise that the three of us have remained close friends for more than twenty-five years.

Of course, I didn't know it or even think about it at the time, but forming lifelong friendships and a mutual support network with this special group of women in the professional sorority was the epitome of "swimming downstream." It all came together naturally, as if it was meant to be. Which it was! When my husband, Larry was diagnosed with congestive heart failure and suffered a fatal heart attack, they were by my side every step of the way. They arrived in full force at his memorial service and continued to hold my hand as I recovered from my loss.

Life offers many gifts as we make our journey. But one of the greatest gifts is the people we meet who have a connection with our Jupiter.

LOVE STORY

He was going to be an actor; she was going to save the world. There was an instant chemistry and attraction. Even though they were young, barely sixteen, they knew they had something special between them. What they didn't know was what life paths were in store for them.

They grew up in a small town in the Midwest. Both went their separate ways after high school. They promised to keep in touch. This was before cell phones, texting and internet were the rage. They continued to meet at holidays and summer vacations, but it soon became apparent that their lives were going in different directions. But even so, they felt this deep-seated bond between them.

You see, her Venus was in the same degree and Sun sign as his Jupiter. This is a very favorable connection between two people. It promotes a peaceful and harmonious relationship. It reduces the couple's feeling of stress and encourages a desire for peace and forgiveness. This is one of the most enduring and loving connections two people can have. The other is when two people have a Sun/Venus connection in their charts.

So not only did they feel very comfortable when they were together, but they could never be mad at each other. But as time passed on, their chosen career paths led them in different directions. He was living in New York and she in Colorado. Eventually she met someone else. They lost contact when she became engaged.

Shortly after she said "I do," she began to feel that something was missing in her marriage, but she could never quite put her finger on it. After 14 years, when Saturn made its difficult aspect in her marriage chart, the marriage could not withstand the pressure. They separated and eventually divorced.

After the dust had settled and she recovered from the emotional trauma of the divorce, she started thinking about her old friend and adolescent sweetheart. Or maybe she never stopped thinking about him. This was also about the time that she was preparing to attend her class reunion. Yes, her special friend with whom she had such a strong Jupiter/Venus connection also attended the reunion.

It was as though no time had passed since they last saw each other. He had never married and she was once again single. They instantly reconnected. Although they still lived miles apart, cell phones and the internet made the distance seem insignificant. Their endearing, enduring friendship and budding romance were once again on track.

SATURN AND THE MARRIAGE CYCLE

They had what appeared to be a perfect marriage. Both were well educated. She was a Libra Sun and he a Gemini Sun. Their strong emphasis of the air signs in their charts indicated their tendency to have the characteristic of being mentally acute, active, social and outgoing. Their lives seemed to be right on track, both with promising careers, an active social life and a beautiful home and family. Gemini, Libra, and Aquarius are known as the air signs. (see Words to Guide You ... Page XII)

They were certainly mentally and intellectually compatible and they parented a very intelligent child. In the beginning they enjoyed the outdoors: hiking, skiing, sailing, jogging. But as with many happy couples, they began to drift apart. The first signs of discontent starting surfacing around the seven-year mark of their marriage. As it turned out, that was also the time that Saturn presented its first difficult aspect in their wedding chart. That difficult aspect is what is called a "Saturn square."

It is not unusual for a marriage to experience challenges at this time. Couples often have to work through issues that have been building over the past seven years. It may present itself as a financial challenge, or as a cycle of discontent. It's a time when a relationship can either become stronger or dissolve. My professional experience over the years has taught me that this is often when someone will seek counseling—or an attorney.

Albert and Wanda survived the first difficult patch,

"the seven year itch," but the next hard Saturn cycle which came seven years later was not going to be so easy. They had both developed very busy lives which seemed to pull them in different directions. Neither of them had found another love interest; they had just drifted apart and became physically incompatible. They knew that their marriage was not working any more.

Interestingly, statistics show that the seven- and fourteen-year marks in a marriage are the most critical. Although they were still friends, they knew they didn't want to be married to each other any longer.

Saturn, the tester and teacher in the chart, tested them to the limit. Fortunately, they were able to draw on their strong Libra and Gemini Suns—Libra being the peacemaker and Gemini the information processor—and were able to maintain a friendship and arbitrate a "friendly divorce." Working through a mediator with no attorneys, they came to an amenable agreement and moved on with their lives. A Saturn cycle doesn't last forever, so take comfort in remembering that we always learn from them and the Saturn cycles help us appreciate the easier, usually more pleasant, Jupiter cycles.

We always seem to remember so vividly the challenging times in our lives, but let's remember to appreciate and enjoy the good times.

"Shoot for the moon and if you miss
you will still be among the stars."

~ Les Brown

Chapter Eight

The Many Faces of the Moon

Smiles, Frowns, and Lives Turned Upside Down

One of my favorite and most reliable astrological timing tools is the lunar cycle. As the Moon travels from new to full it can be a tremendous aid for planning and timing events. The lunar and solar eclipses are especially "event significant." The lunar cycle can give you a tremendous edge in your professional and personal life. It is without a doubt one of the major factors that is available in timing events to achieve your desired results.

Following the lunar cycle each month is just like having your own personal GPS for your journey through life. The lunar cycle can be used in timing your activities and is one of the most valuable tools you can use. In many Eastern countries, timing by the planets is so important that practically no event takes place without first setting up an astrological chart. Many times weddings take place in the middle of the night because that is when the planetary influences are the most favorable.

Since ancient times the cycle of the Moon from new to full to new has been observed and correlated with events on Earth. The early farmers learned that sowing seed at the New Moon leads to better harvest. Sailors learned to time their travels by the phase of the Moon, which everyone knows controls the tides. In addition to controlling the tides, the Moon rules the ebb and flow of the bodily fluids, emotions, feelings and state of mind.

FISHING AND THE MOON

Living at the ocean has given me first-hand knowledge of the trends of the fishing boats during the fishing season. Saltwater fishing is an occupation—or hobby—with a lot of self-anointed "experts" who often disagree with each other on just about everything, but catch records of professionals, recreational anglers and scientific studies say that saltwater species are more active for four days leading up to the Full Moon and for four days after the New Moon. There are other variables to consider, like water temperature and time of day, but when the Moon is full the trolling fishing boats light up the horizon like a Christmas tree. The tides are noticeably higher during the new and full phases of the Moon and the increased movement of water may hold the explanation for why the fish seem more active at this time.

STORM PATTERNS

At the New Moon, the Sun and Moon are together in the heavens creating a massive concentration of energy, which can lead to the development of strong storm systems. This can be an emotional storm or a full blown hurricane. Think about how you feel when there is a Full Moon. Energy levels tend to run higher, less sleep is needed. The New Moon is the time to plant the seeds that you will harvest during the Full Moon.

Although the New Moon and the Full Moon and the few days leading up to them are the strongest times in the cycle, the total lunar cycle needs to be taken into consideration when timing an event or project. As I mentioned earlier, following the lunar cycle each month can be just like having a personal GPS to help you with your journey through life. It is a day-to-day guide for planning your actions, and paying close attention to it will help you to better achieve your desired goals. Eclipse cycles can also add a strong impact on the weather, but that's the subject of my next chapter.

You will want to pay special attention if there is a storm approaching during a New or Full Moon. A perfect example that comes to mind is the series of hurricanes that hit Florida in 2004. I can still recall the weather forecast for the approaching storm as I was observing its daily movement in relation to the lunar cycle. We were approaching the New Moon of August 16 when Hurricane Charley, having come ashore on Florida's West Coast a little south of Tampa, was predicted to travel across the state and hit the East Coast of Florida.

We pulled down the shutters on our condo and battened the hatches for what proved to be a thrashing, nightmare of a storm. In the pitch black of the night we could hear the shrieking sounds as the eye of the storm reached us and rushed over us. It has been said so often but it's true: it sounded like a fast moving train rolling over our head. We were one of the few residents in the building who chose to stay and weather the storm.

I had survived Karen, a 210 knot typhoon when I lived on Guam, an island in the Pacific, while my father was stationed there in the Navy. I wasn't about to be chased out of my home by a hurricane that may or may not come our way. But it certainly did come our way. It was a doozy. Everyone in our building who did not have hurricane shutters lost their windows and sliding glass doors. Their interiors were left in shambles. All of the condo units located under these vulnerable units were also flooded as the water made its way through the ceilings and walls.

It seems that the condominium building located next to ours had a flat pebble roof and the pebbles where jetted through the air like bullets, destroying every window pane that was not covered. Fortunately, our shutters saved us. Fortunately, our neighbors above us also had shutters which prevented us from being flooded from above. We were one of the few units that did not suffer water damage. Our storm shutters looked like they had been riveted with buckshot.

When we poked our heads out the door after the storm moved on, the parking lot looked like a war zone. There was furniture, debris and glass everywhere. It felt like we were in a bombed out, evacuated city and we were the only living souls around. It was devastating and brought back my childhood memories of typhoon Karen. In addition to the structural damage of the storm, the erosion of the shoreline was disastrous and heartbreaking.

Just three weeks later on September 8, 2004, hurricane Frances was forecast to be heading our way. Of course we thought, no way, not again. When it seemed that "again" really was going to happen, I referred to my astrological calendar. This time the storm was six days prior to the September 14 New Moon, so I figured it would not be as devastating. We chose to stay, battening down the hatches once again. The biggest problem was that people had not had time to repair their roofs from the last hurricane and the water had not had time to seep into the ground. Unfortunately, the already damaged shoreline was getting another unneeded beating.

As if that were not enough, on September 26, 2004, hurricane Jeanne struck us. The Full Moon was September 28. She alone was not as destructive as hurricanes Charley and Frances, but she certainly added to the already disastrous situation. There was already way too much water and not enough time to repair roofs in between these lunar cycles. Of course, it goes without saying that we—and most of our neighboring communities—were without electricity for days or weeks. Some people didn't even get their electric turned back on before the next storm hit.

"OBSERVING THE MOON AS IT TRAVELS FROM ONE SIGN TO THE NEXT IS LIKE READING YOUR PERSONAL BAROMETER ..."

The lesson to this story is that you may want to consider evacuating if there is a major storm predicted to be heading your way around the time of a Full or New Moon. You can't stop it but you can get out of its way.

WAR STRATEGIES

On May 2, 2011, the United States Special Forces launched a successful, strategical attack on Osama bin Laden, the terrorist leader who was thought to be the mastermind behind the 9/11 "Twin Towers" attack. I thought it was very interesting that this attack took place during the balsamic "dark of the Moon" cycle. Then I heard on the news that the military leaders planned this deliberately so that the low-flying helicopters bringing in the troops would not be spotted. This strategy of using the dark of the Moon goes back to ancient times. This strategy was discussed in "Art of War" by Sun Tzu, a Chinese military commander from 6th century BC. I found it to be very interesting that we are still using the same war tactics today that were used more than 2500 years ago in ancient China. Our modern day war strategists are still coordinating with the lunar cycle. Not that any of us are planning to go to war, I just thought this to be an interesting bit of information to share with you. Let your mind drift a bit and maybe you'll imagine some special "caper" that would be more successful if carried out under the balsamic Moon—but please, don't do anything illegal!

SUPER FULL MOON DOG TROUBLE

Some of us may find ourselves unknowingly in a war zone. Much to my dismay, I can recall a traumatic experience which serves as a perfect example to illustrate the influence of the planets in action. For months my neighbors and I had been enduring another neighbor's barking dog. Finally, one day I had enough of listening to it. But instead of calling the police or animal control I decided to pay a visit to the neighbor to make a personal appeal. This was not a good idea, even under the best of circumstances.

Unfortunately, the woman who owned the troublesome dog was not the neighborly type and did not appreciate the neighborly visit. She became very defensive when I informed her that the entire neighborhood was upset over her dog's incessant barking. And then the woman who owned the German Shepherd physically attacked me and yelled at me. Thankfully, the dog behaved itself, but had I stopped and thought better of my timing I probably could have avoided this incident. There was a "Super Full Moon" approaching and emotions run extremely high during this time. It most definitely was not the best time to approach my neighbor.

Even when we are consciously aware of what is going on, our emotions can take over. Although I knew we were approaching a Super Full Moon, I allowed my emotions to get the best of me in spite of my better judgment. Or maybe the Super Full Moon is what pushed me over the edge.

A Super Full Moon is a rare occasion. The last one was 20 years prior. It is referred to as a "Super Full Moon" because the Moon appears much larger and is much closer to the earth, thereby creating a greater force of energy on the earth. This will intensify the emotional influence for us living here on earth.

I learned that shortly after that incident, the German Shepherd, which was a beautiful dog, was sent to obedience school. It was no surprise that this very intelligent breed that is used by law enforcement agencies was quickly taught to stop barking by using hand commands. The neighborhood was once again quiet, so something good did come of the neighbors' war. Fortunately, there were no charges pressed, but neither would there be any Christmas gifts exchanged.

The Moon can often be read like an emotional barometer, and some people tend to be even more emotionally affected by the lunar cycle than others.

For example, people who have their Sun or Moon in the sign of Cancer tend to be especially sensitive to the lunar cycles. Also, someone who has a Cancer ascendant, meaning that the sign of Cancer was on the horizon at the time of their birth, tend to be very sensitive and emotional and also vulnerable to the lunar cycles.

YOUR LUNAR GPS: A NAVIGATION TOOL

You can easily learn to use the cycles of the Moon to help plan your activities so that you can enjoy optimum results. Most calendars provide this information. Of course, astrological calendars provide more in-depth information.

New Moon – When the Moon is traveling 0-45 degrees ahead of the Sun it is considered to be in its new phase. This is an excellent time to begin anything that you would want to have longevity. It is considered to be the germination cycle. This is an excellent time for putting ideas into action by initiating and outwardly directing your activities.

There is a direct correlation between what is already happening in your life and how you will feel and react to the energy of the New Moon. You may enjoy feelings of rest and peace if all is going well; or chaos, disorganization and confusion if your life is already in turmoil. Whichever is the case, whatever you initiate during this cycle should be fruitful. Just be careful. If you choose to do something harmful—for example, to initiate a campaign of revenge against someone—it may get out of hand. If you choose to begin a positive endeavor, it is likely to blossom. I chose this cycle to begin writing this book.

It is best to avoid elective surgery during this phase of the Moon, as there will tend to be more bleeding.

First Quarter or Waxing Moon – (seven days following the New Moon) When the Moon is 90-135 degrees ahead of the Sun it is still considered to be in the growth and development phase and activities that apply to the New Moon cycle also apply to the Waxing Moon.

Second Quarter – When the Moon is approximately 140–175 degrees ahead of the Sun the energy and activity is a continuation of the 1st quarter activities.

Third Quarter or Full Moon – (fourteen days following the New Moon) When the Moon is 180 degrees from the Sun it is considered to be in its maturity or fruition phase. This is when you will see the fruits of your labor and the seeds that you have planted during a New Moon cycle come to fruition. Emotions tend to run high. Depending upon what is going on in your life, you may feel ecstatic or depressed. Feelings and emotions tend to be exaggerated when the Moon is full. Elective surgery should also be avoided during this phase of the Moon as there tends to be more bleeding and swelling.

It has been my experience that people often times require less sleep or have difficulty sleeping a couple of nights before the Full Moon. Since energy levels tend to be higher, this is an excellent time to escalate your exercise program. You should be able to accomplish a great deal during this lunar cycle

Fourth Quarter or Waning Moon – (seven days following the Full Moon) When the Moon is traveling 90–135 degrees behind the Sun it is in its disintegration and drawing back phase. This is the time for reorganization, rest and reflection. This is when you will want to step back and get the big picture, to regroup and analyze your progress with initiatives you have already begun.

Balsamic Moon or Dark of the Moon – (fourteen days following the Full Moon) This is the 24-hour period just before the New Moon. During this phase of the Moon the Sun's light is not reflective. It is *not* a good time to initiate any projects that you would want to produce long-term results. This is also *not* the best time to be making new contacts, especially if you happen to work in the field of sales or marketing. This is also not the preferred time to sign contracts or legal documents as there may be a lack of clarity, or an inability to follow through.

This should be a quiet, working behind the scenes time. It is best to avoid high expectations, major decisions or physical projects. You will want to focus on mental tasks for the best use of your time on these days. This is a great time to plan and prepare for what you want to do when the Moon is new. Energy levels tend to run low during this cycle, so it's better not to push yourself.

THE MOON TRAVELING THROUGH THE SUN SIGNS

This is another tool that can be used to help you plan your activities in order to achieve a result that you'll appreciate.

I have found it to be very helpful to pay attention to the sign that the Moon is traveling through each day, as this can be a tremendous aid in helping you plan your activities. For example, when the Moon is in the sign of Virgo it is an excellent time for doing activities that require attention to details.

Since it takes the Moon two and a half days to travel through each Sun sign there is ample time for all activities in the course of a month. The Moon's movement through each of its signs can be followed easily with an astrological calendar.

It is also important to note on an astrological calendar that period of time when the Moon is *void of course*. The Moon is V/C (*void of course*) when it makes its last major aspect with another planet before going into the next sign. An aspect is the same as a connection to another planet. For example, the planet may be in the same degree and sign as the Moon or even opposite the Moon. It remains *void of course* until it enters a new sign, in which it will make another aspect. An astrological aspect refers to the relationship or connection between the planets.

During the V/C period it is advisable not to make any major decisions or sign contracts. It would be best not to start anything that you want to be long lasting. Think of it as a balsamic or dark of the Moon cycle. This can last for as little as a few minutes or up to several hours. Again, an astrological calendar will be instrumental in helping you chart your course.

It has been my experience that when the Moon is *void of course* it is very difficult to bring anything to completion, or even accomplish something as simple as reaching someone on the phone.

Observing the Moon as it travels from one sign to the next is like reading your personal barometer and acting accordingly. A barometer measures the barometric pressure in the atmosphere. It lets us know when the pressure is dropping and therefore rain is forthcoming. With that knowledge you can plan your activities more effectively. You probably would not want to schedule a picnic when the barometer is dropping. In the same way, as the Moon is traveling through each sign you can take advantage by timing your activities as they relate to the sign and task at hand.

THE MOON'S JOURNEY THROUGH THE SIGNS

When the Moon is traveling through the sign of **Aries** it is an excellent time to be an initiator. It is a positive time to start a new job or project. This is especially true when a New Moon is in Aries, but be careful—tempers tend to run hot and patience can be short. I would suggest not doing anything that might create confrontation. I've noticed that drivers tend to be more aggressive and impatient during this lunar cycle.

When the Moon is traveling through the sign of **Taurus** you will find your focus and attention drawn toward reinforcing your values and sense of security. You may spend this time balancing your checkbook or paying bills. You will want to evaluate what is really important to you. This is a good time to begin anything that you want to have longevity. For example, open a new savings account or start a new business venture. It is also a wonderful time to plant a garden, especially if it is a New Moon.

When the Moon is traveling through the sign of **Gemini** you will be drawn toward mental and expressive activities. You may find yourself drawn to reading, writing, exploring new areas of knowledge, and wanting to communicate more. You may also have a sudden wish to take a short trip, or just to get yourself in motion by running errands around town. Your desire is to expand your horizons, but you will need to prioritize because there is a tendency to become scattered.

When the Moon is in the sign of **Cancer** it is in its comfortable placement. This is a perfect time for nurturing. You will be more interested in domestic activities, particularly if your natal Sun or Moon is in the sign of Cancer. You will be drawn to spending more time at home and taking care of family matters. Don't be surprised if you feel an impulse to spend time in your kitchen trying out some new recipes.

The period when the Moon is in **Leo** is a time to let the child in you come out and play. You will want to be artistic, romantic and creative. You will enjoy going to a movie, a play, a concert, or out to dinner. This could be a good time to play the lottery or go to Las Vegas, especially if other aspects in your chart are set up well to support this.

When the Moon is in the sign of **Virgo** it is a great time to get organized—particularly if Mercury is retrograde. You will feel motivated to take care of details, like cleaning out closets and drawers and your desk. You will want to take care of health matters such as doctor's appointments, health check-ups and physicals. If it happens to be a "new" Moon in Virgo it is a great time to begin a diet or exercise program.

When the Moon is in the sign of **Libra** it is an excellent time for negotiating and dealing with others on a one-to-one basis. For instance, you are likely to have that heart-to-heart talk you have been putting off with your spouse or co-worker. Since this is typically a non-confrontational time, the outcome should be fruitful. This can be a time to enjoy the peace and harmony you have been seeking in your life.

The Moon in the sign of **Scorpio** can be a very strong emotional time. This is not a good time for confrontation, especially if it is a Full Moon. People often feel secretive or less communicative during this cycle. It is a good time for regenerative actions and investigative work. You can get to the bottom of things, and loose ends dangling in the back of your mind can finally be tied off. Insurance questions, or legal matters like a will, may need to be taken care of. This is a good time to do so.

When the Moon is in the sign of **Sagittarius** it is a

good time for spiritual development and philosophical thought. You may be motivated to enroll in a college course, or to continue or start a new line of study. This is a great time to begin a long trip or vacation. People tend to feel upbeat and optimistic during this cycle. It is a good time to open yourself up without apprehension or prior expectations and see what flows in.

The Moon in the sign of **Capricorn** is a good time to become organized and bring structure into your life. People tend to be more critical during this cycle. This is the time that you will want to take care of business. It is a no-nonsense time. Your time is better spent working than playing.

When the Moon is in the sign of **Aquarius** it is an excellent time for socializing, particularly if Venus is making a favorable aspect in your chart. It is great for attending club or organization activities, and parties. There is a tendency to be more creative and open minded during this cycle.

The Moon in the sign of **Pisces** is a good time for enhancing spiritual development. You will want to get in touch with your inner emotions. People will tend to be more compassionate and in tune to other people's feelings. There is also a tendency to have your feelings hurt more easily, especially if your natal Sun or Moon is in this sign.

It is especially important to observe the sign that the Moon is in when there is an eclipse, as this magnifies the activities and makes them even more significant.

*"It's only during an eclipse that the
Man in the Moon has a place in the Sun"*

~ Unknown

CHAPTER NINE

ECLIPSES: THE GREAT MAGNIFIER

THE MOON ON STEROIDS

If the Moon transiting through the Sun signs is like a barometer, eclipses are a time to pay even closer attention to what the barometer is reading. These are times of revelation in the sense that you can see more clearly how and where the pressure is going to affect your life. When there is an eclipse, the result is an even stronger lunar energy of the various types described in the previous chapter. Whatever is going on in your life is magnified.

For example, I can recall a client who was experiencing a lunar eclipse in his 12th house.

The 12th house is the area of the chart that deals with being confined or having to take care of someone who is confined. Many times when a person experiences an eclipse in this area of their chart, they are either admitted to the hospital, have to visit someone who is in the hospital or take care of someone who is sick. In his case he found out that he was going to have rotator cuff surgery which required a hospital stay.

I can also vividly recall when I experienced a lunar eclipse in my 12th house. My mother was admitted to the hospital and I spent a great deal of time there as a visitor. This particular hospital played the lullaby song throughout the hospital every time a baby was born. It seemed like there was a baby born every five minutes. I couldn't help chuckling to myself as I connected it to the activities that were going on in the sky.

After her release from the hospital my mother went to a rehabilitation facility, another confinement, where I played a major role as her care giver. Yes, I did see this coming in my chart and I was not surprised when this sequence of events took place.

"OFTENTIMES WE BEGIN TO SEE AND FEEL THE EFFECTS OF AN ECLIPSE A MONTH OR SO PRIOR TO THE ACTUAL DATE OF THE ECLIPSE."

We can feel and see the effects of the Full Moon every month: emotions run high, tides are higher, the emergency rooms are busier and more babies are born. But when a Full Moon corresponds with a lunar eclipse, be prepared to seize the moment, play it careful, or expect the unexpected, as the case may be. No matter what is happening, for good or for ill, emotions and events are significantly magnified.

A DEEPER LOOK AT THE ECLIPSE FACTOR

In case I haven't said this clearly enough, I want to repeat that every influence in astrology must be viewed in connection with other factors. For instance, while the influence of the Moon passing through each Sun sign has meaning for everyone, the strength of those influences can vary based on a person's natal chart. Eclipses are another variable.

When following the lunar cycle from new to full each month, it is especially important to pay attention to the eclipse cycles. The lunar and solar eclipses can be instrumental in the timing of life-changing events.

This is particularly significant if the eclipse happens to fall on or near your Sun sign or opposite your Sun sign. For example, if an eclipse takes place in the sign of Aries and you are an Aries Sun sign, it will signal a significant year for you. There has been a great deal of debate as to how long the effects of an eclipse last. It has been my personal experience that we can begin to see the effects of an eclipse as early as thirty days prior and as long as a year after the actual event.

There are two sets of eclipse patterns each year which take place six months apart. This is a technical description of eclipses, according to various sources: A *solar eclipse* takes place when there is a full or partial obscuring of the Sun by the Moon. A *lunar eclipse* happens when the Sun, Moon and earth are all in alignment with each other. The moon is blocked by the earth from reaching the sun.

A solar eclipse, when the Sun and Moon are together in the sky, is a wonderful time for initiating or embracing the new. The lunar eclipse, when the Sun and Moon are opposite each other, is a time when that which is hidden will be brought out into the light. It is a time of illumination.

There are many excellent books written about this subject; my personal favorite is the classic, *Interpreting the Eclipses* by Robert Carl Jansky. A more recent publication which I also found to be very enlightening is *Eclipses* by Celeste Teal.

A FEARFUL TIME FOR THE ANCIENTS

In ancient times it was thought that eclipses were malefic because the people simply didn't understand what was happening. They knew only that the Sun was covered and it had become dark in the middle of the day. Since they were unable to correlate this to a natural event—a solar eclipse—they became fearful.

There is a reading from the Bible describing the crucifixion of Jesus that refers to the sky becoming dark at noon as he died on the cross. Christian tradition has always interpreted this unusual event as God—or the heavens—commenting on what had happened. Like most ancient people, those who witnessed the event didn't understand eclipses, so they attributed it to supernatural intervention. On the other hand, scholars have often pondered how the death of some obscure prophet in a backwater corner of civilization produced a worldwide religion. Could the presence of a powerful eclipse at the time of his death have had an influence on what happened afterward, or on the timing of when it happened? One can't help but wonder if it was just coincidence that Jesus' crucifixion took place during a solar eclipse.

A CASE STUDY IN ECLIPSES: "ROCKY MOUNTAIN HIGH"

John Denver is one of my all time favorite musical artists. I grew up listening to his music. I fell in love to "Annie's Song" and dreamed of some day seeing the "Rocky Mountain Highs." His "County Boy" style warmed my soul and was endearing to my heart. I attended every concert

that was within one hundred miles of me and even man-
aged to see him when I was on vacation in San Diego one
time. I just couldn't get enough of his music. I listened to
him when I was cleaning house on Saturday morning and
driving to work on Monday morning.

The shocking news of his death was devastating. I
felt like I had lost a member of my family. As a part of my
therapy in dealing with his death I began researching and
studying his life and his astrology chart. I found it to be
a perfect case study since the patterns of his success related to the astrological cycles that were taking place in his
life. I was particularly fascinated by how the eclipse cycles
had affected the timing of his success and the peak of his
popularity.

John Denver's greatest commercial success as a solo
singer was from 1971 to 1975. Throughout his life Denver
recorded and released approximately three hundred
songs, about two hundred of which he composed. He per-
formed primarily with an acoustic guitar and sang about
his joy in nature, his enthusiasm for music and his relationship trials. Denver's music appeared on a variety of charts
including country and western, the Billboard Hot 100,
and adult contemporary, earning him 12 gold and four
platinum albums with his signature songs, "Take Me Home
Country Roads," "Rocky Mountain High," "Annie's Song,"
and "Calypso." He also starred in films and several notable
television specials in the 1970s and 1980s. It's fair to say
that Denver will always be remembered as one of the most
popular—and best—acoustic artists of the 1970s. His re-
nown in the State of Colorado, which he sang about numerous times and where he lived in Aspen, influenced the
governor to name him Poet Laureate of the state in 1974.
The state legislature adopted "Rocky Mountain High" as

one of Colorado's state songs in 2007.

John Denver released his first RCA album in 1969 and followed with another in 1970, neither of which was a commercial success. It was not until 1971 that "Take Me Home Country Roads" became his first number one hit. Not surprisingly, this is also when the triple eclipses in 1971 made a major impact in his astrology chart. It was at this time that he began his rapidly escalating climb toward the apex of his success. The Lunar Eclipse that took place in Leo on February 10, 1971 was in close relationship to his natal Jupiter. Jupiter is the planet that rules creative, philosophic writing and publications. It also rules expansion, growth and optimism. Whenever there is an eclipse that falls on or near a person's natal Jupiter it can set off a very positive sequence of events for the individual, which can have a rippling effect that will carry over for several years into the future.

On February 25, 1971, John Denver's 10th house was the recipient of a solar eclipse. The 10th house, as you may recall, represents your public image, your dealings with the public, and your career. It is the very public part of your chart where there are typically no secrets. And John certainly did become a very public figure in 1971.

John was already a talented and charismatic writer-composer, but he was about to become very widely known. Although his beautiful lyrics and music pushed him into the light, there was something more that catapulted him toward national celebrity. The February 10, 1971 Lunar Eclipse was certainly a catalyst in of itself, but then on July 22, 1971 there was a Solar Eclipse that took place in his 3rd house of writing and mental acuity. If you remember, the Lunar Eclipse is typically when we see the results of labor come to fruition. But wait, there's more. It gets even better.

In August of that same year there were two more life alter-ing eclipses in John Denver's astrology chart.

On August 6,1971 there was a Lunar Eclipse that took place in his 9th house of creative philosophic writing and publication. This is also the house that Jupiter rules. As you may recall, every house has a ruling planet and an area of life that it influences. So he was getting a double whammy of some good positive Jupiter energy.

But there was more to come. On August 20, 1971 there was a Solar Eclipse which took place exactly on John's natal Jupiter. This really set his career into high gear. Little did he know that it was his destiny to feel and live the energy of these eclipses for many years to come. Of course, being who he was, maybe he did know.

A CASE STUDY: TIGER WOODS STORY

It has long been my belief that the best way to help people understand is by telling a story to illustrate your point. So here is one more. This is a true life example of how an eclipse can make a major impact on a person's life. Tiger Woods was born with his Sun in the sign of Capricorn on December 30, 1975. On December 31, 2009 there was a lunar eclipse in the sign of Cancer directly opposite his Sun. On November 27, 2009, just prior to this lunar eclipse, Tiger Woods experienced a life-changing event. He had an automobile accident in front of his home. Although the eclipse was not to take place until December 31, the building energy of this powerful lunation was already in motion.

Although what took place behind the scenes is still a mystery to the general public, shortly following the December 31 lunar eclipse (remember, lunar eclipses bring information to light) the news of his "indiscretions" became public knowledge. This was very timely as it directly related to what was going on in his astrological chart.

This lunar eclipse took place in his 10th house of career and public image. Anything that he was doing behind the scenes would likely come out in the open and affect his public image. Had he consulted an astrologer he would have learned that there was going to be a major focus on his public image in 2010. It bears repeating that although astrology does not predict the future it can help prepare us for our pitfalls and shortcomings. It helps us to make better decisions in our life. The use of the lunar cycles— and especially the eclipse cycle—can be invaluable for planning and timing events, and for avoiding what is un-desirable.

LIFE CHANGING ECLIPSE — THE FORTUITOUS ECLIPSE

Oftentimes we begin to see and feel the effects of an eclipse a month or so prior to the actual date of the eclipse. I can recall working with a Gemini client who was in the process of selling an estate house. When he inherited the house it was in need of a great deal of work, so he was very skeptical about it being a quick and easy sale. He put the house on the market in February with little hope of finding a buyer before the maintenance issues became a burden.

After studying his chart, I noticed that the solar eclipse was going to take place on his Gemini Sun, indicating that there would probably be life changing events taking place for him sooner, rather then later. I suggested that he would find a buyer and probably close on the house right around his birthday, the end of May. This would indeed make a major impact on his life and free him from a burdensome situation. As it turned out the planets were aligned very nicely for him and he actually closed on the house four weeks prior to the eclipse. It is a measure of the magnifying power of eclipses that they can significantly influence events for so long before and after the actual eclipse date.

"The past is dead. The future is imaginary.
Happiness can only be in the Eternal now moment."

Ken Keyes Jr. **Handbook to Higher Consciousness**

CHAPTER TEN

HER WINTER OF DISCONTENT

IT CAN GET COMPLICATED

It was two days before her 68th birthday—which also happened to be the week before Christmas—when her husband walked in the door and said, "I want a divorce." You could have knocked her over with a feather. She could feel the sting in her cheeks, like he had slapped her across the face. The wind was completely gone from her lungs. She couldn't breathe. She was in shock. Although she knew after thirty-five years that her marriage was not one of those that people say are "made in heaven," it was *her* marriage and the only one she had.

The children were long gone. She cooked and took care of the house, and he went to the office every day. They were co-existing. There were no fights, no arguments. Life was just life, plodding along. That is, until it changed.

After she picked herself up and dusted herself off, she said, "What do you mean you want a divorce?" Nothing that he said made much sense and she was too numb to even remember or recall any of the conversation after the words, "I want a divorce."

Her next conscious action was to pick up the phone and call me. "What in the word is going on in my astrology chart?" she asked. I could hear her sobbing into the phone. So I quickly ran her chart on my computer software. This gave me the full picture as to where all of the planets were in relationship to her chart, which was reflected in her life. It was all there. Hindsight may be 20/20, but there is a lot to be said for gaining a little foresight to help us through a crisis.

> "WE CHARTED A NEW COURSE FOR THE NEXT COUPLE OF YEARS, KNOWING FULL WELL THAT THIS WAS NOT JUST A PASSING THUNDER STORM; IT WAS A FULL BLOWN HURRICANE."

Saturn, the planet which is the tester and teacher, was coming up to her ascendant, which is your window to the world and your physical body. Her outlook on the world was certainly going to be tested and she was going to learn a great deal. It just so happened that Saturn was also making a connection to her natal Uranus, the planet that is known for erratic and unexpected events. And this event was like a lightning bolt out of the blue.

At this same time Pluto—the transformer—was beginning his journey into her 4th house of home and family matters, while at the same time making a nasty aspect to Saturn. Yes, her home was certainly going to be transformed. In fact, her whole life was going to be transformed and this was just the beginning of her transformation. Unfortunately, it was a journey that was going to continue for another twelve years. Her chart indicated that she would probably move several times during this transformation cycle, and/or her residence would be remodeled. There would be changes taking place within her family.

These planetary transits, in and of themselves, would have been very challenging, but there was more to come. On New Year's Eve of that same year, there was a lunar eclipse that took place in her 10th house. This is the house that represents your public persona, and your connection to the outside world—the public. It is also opposite the 4th house where a solar eclipse took place two weeks later. Her image and public persona were certainly going to change. At this point there was no way to avoid it. She was going to be divorced after thirty-five years of living with and taking care of this man. Her home and family matters— her entire life it seemed—was being turned upside down.

As if things were not bad enough, it was also during the time when these eclipses were taking place that she discovered that her husband of so many years had been having an affair for God knows how long. Eclipses do have a way of bringing information out into the light.

The information she acquired from her astrology chart couldn't change her charted course, but it did help her to understand what was going on. It helped her to plan and prepare for a future without this man. She shared with me that it was a relief to know that this cycle was going to run its course and life would eventually be normal again—whatever normal was now going to be.

We charted a new course for the next couple of years, knowing full well that this was not just a passing thunder storm; it was a full blown hurricane. And she needed all of the help and support that I could give her.

The divorce came to pass, but life was still unsettling

for her. We had discussed the fact that the planetary cycle she was experiencing was slow moving. So she knew that she had a long road to travel. A year-and-a-half after her husband announced that he wanted a divorce, her mother passed away. Although there is no way to predict death in a chart—nor would any ethical astrologer try to—there can be planetary indications showing illnesses and challenges, particularly when it is a close family member.

Although it is impossible to tell exactly what is going to take place, there are indicators—like when Saturn was coming into my 4th house many years earlier and Brenda told me that I would probably be taking care of one of my parents that year. That was the year that my father had a heart attack and I did take care of him. She did not predict that he was going to have a heart attack, but her counseling certainly helped me deal with the crisis when it arose.

I received another call from my now divorced client shortly after her mother's passing. It was no surprise that this call came on the heels of a solar eclipse in Cancer which took place in her 10th house. The 4th and 10th houses are also known as the parental axis. She was once again feeling the same sense of loss and despair as when her husband shocked her with his decision to seek a divorce. But she knew that this too would pass. She had been through these life changing eclipses before and she knew she would survive. She was a tough and resilient lady. She was strong and she would survive. She had learned through our sessions that this cycle would soon become history, and there were some really nice Jupiter aspects that would be coming her way in a few months.

"Relationships, we all got 'em, we all want 'em.
What do we do with them?"

~ Jimmy Buffett

CHAPTER ELEVEN
SECRET KEYS TO RELATIONSHIPS
TIME IS OF THE ESSENCE

Statistics indicate that about fifty percent of all first marriages fail, but are you aware the divorce rates of second marriages are estimated to be over seventy percent? Maybe this explains why many people end up married three and four times before they find that person to grow old with until "death do us part."

I have learned over the past thirty years of studying and practicing astrology that timing is one of the key ingredients in the success of any relationship and/or friendship. And astrology can be a key tool to help you understand and use the correct timing. I feel certain that if I had met my current husband twenty years earlier it would not have worked because it would not have been the right time. We were not the same people then as we were when we met. I would not have appreciated him, nor would he have appreciated me.

It has been my experience that the secret of finding a good relationship is all about the intersection of "timing" and "compatibility." And we tend to be more compatible if we meet someone "when the time is right." To paraphrase the Cialis commercial, "will you be ready when the time is right?"

Some people go from one relationship to another, attracting the same type of person over and over again. As the saying goes: "If you keep doing the same thing, you'll keep getting the same results."

Some people always seem to attract people that are not good for them or are emotionally unavailable. And others find life becomes much simpler if they avoid having a relationship. This decision can be make on a conscious or subconscious level, while still others sabotage their relationships—either consciously or subconsciously.

People change and what they want in a relationship also changes. Some people change for the better and grow together, but unfortunately in our society many people seem to grow apart.

Right times and wrong times:

Avoid falling into a new relationship immediately after a break up—

We all have heard—or maybe given—that advice. But how many times have you seen someone who has just gone through a divorce turn around and within a short period of time marry the very same type of person again? And perhaps even do it a third time.

Let's face it; most people do not want to be alone. We're all looking for love and companionship, but let's give the planets a chance to change positions before we run out and hitch up with another *"ditto"* that is absolutely like the one we just divorced. If we remarry under the same planetary aspects that we divorced under it is a continuation of where we left off. That doesn't sound like much fun to me. (Planetary aspect refers to where the planets were positioned in the sky at the time of the event.)

So, here's that classic bit of advice once more: "Wait at least a year after a divorce before you jump into a serious relationship." This sounds to me like good, solid, common-sense advice. And the stars back it up.

The New Moon is a wonderful time to begin a new relationship—

Typically, anything which you initiate or begin on the New Moon will have a long and lasting life span. I can recall referring to my astrological calendar when my future husband, a blind date, called to ask me out for the first time. I suggested we meet on a day when there happened to be a "New Moon."

Relationships, especially new relationships, have a definite life cycle—

A new relationship has a definite cycle and pattern. Anyone who has been on the dating scene will know exactly what I'm talking about. In the beginning it's very mysterious and exciting. The beginning that I am referring to lasts about three months. In the third month, the Moon moves to a ninety degree angle, which is a square to where it was when you first starting dating.

This is generally when the complexion of the relationship begins to change. It can become more intimate or it can just go away. The newness has worn off—that is unless it is a long-distance relationship, in which case this does not apply in the same way. Long distance romances usu-

85

ally take much longer to develop or go away. But for most, the three-month mark is typically when the relationship either ends or climbs to the next level. This is generally when people think seriously about whether they want to invest any more time or energy with this person.

The next plateau is the six-month time period. This is when the Moon has reached its opposition, which means it is 180 degrees from where it was when you began the relationship. This is the second critical point in the relationship cycle.

At the end of the first year, which is when the Moon will return to where it was when you first began dating, if you are still together, you will have completed the first cycle of your relationship. If you've made it this far, this first cycle was probably a blooming and blossoming season for your relationship. I can certainly see how people might want to jump into marriage during this blooming cycle, especially if they are young and have never been married before. But this cycle should have an opportunity to complete itself before thinking about making a commitment.

Be careful if transiting Uranus is conjunct with your natal Venus when you meet someone—

There I go again talking that other language. To review in simple English: Uranus is the planet that is known for its erratic and unexpected behavior. Venus is known for inspiring love and romance. Conjunct means being together. Transiting means the planet is moving across the sky. Natal refers to where the planet was at the time of you birth.

So when traveling across the sky, Uranus comes together with your natal Venus there is usually an erratic, unexpected love affair that is short-lived. You will want to be careful of this if you are already in a committed relationship, as it can be very destructive. Anyone who has experienced this will know exactly what I am referring to.

One case study that comes to mind involves a client who had been happily married for many years to a wonderful man. When transiting Uranus connected with her natal Venus she became strongly attracted to her next door neighbor, a man she had always thought to be handsome but had never before considered as a possible lover. She had never even gone so far as to imagine herself expressing her feelings to him or taking action on her thoughts. Although she had always felt that there was a spark between them, they were both happily married after all, so neither of them would ever encourage it. They were just friendly neighbors.

But this Uranus/Venus connection was almost more than she could handle. Fortunately, she was very aware of what was going on astrologically so she was forearmed. No action was taken and she made a special point to stay away from the neighbor during this cycle. When Uranus moved away from her Venus, life and her emotions returned to normal. She realized in retrospect what a horrible mistake she could have made had she not understood what was really going on.

PAST LOVES/NEW LOVES

Venus, the ruler and Goddess of Love, stations retrograde every eighteen months and continues on its retrograde path for approximately six weeks. In simple English, retrograde means that the planet is traveling in an apparent backward motion and is not operating on all of its cylinders.

This can be a wild and crazy time for romantic relationships. This is when counselors are really busy. It is the time when love energy is really intensified. A love or loves from the past can come back into your life. One of my clients reconnected with her high school sweetheart while attending her class reunion during a Venus retrograde cycle.

I can remember the thrill of it when I was single. I always got excited when Venus went retrograde. I knew that some kind of adventure—or the memory of one—would soon materialize. I would run into or get a call from guys that I hadn't heard from in ages. Or I'd start thinking about someone and then he'd call.

> "I EXPLAINED TO HER THAT TIMING IS EVERYTHING AND IT REALLY DOESN'T MATTER WHERE YOU LIVE OR WHAT YOU DO. WHEN THE TIME IS RIGHT IT JUST HAPPENS."

A relationship can be very important and meaningful if you meet someone and start the relationship when Venus is starting to travel in its direct motion again.

If you happen to start a relationship during a Venus retrograde cycle, it can be difficult for you to express loving, caring and comfortable feelings for someone. It is typically a relationship that will not endure. Even a solid love relationship can be tried and tested during this cycle. Attempts to communicate feelings of the heart can be misunderstood. People tend to be more insecure in matters of the heart when Venus is traveling in retrograde motion. Knowing this can alert a couple that a little extra sensitivity may be required.

LEARN FROM THE PAST, PLAN FOR THE FUTURE ~
Dates to remember and plan accordingly—

Venus was traveling in retrograde motion from *October 8, 2010* to *November 18, 2010*. Venus will be traveling in retrograde motion from *May 15, 2012* to *Ju 2012*; from *December 21, 2013* to *January 31, 2014*, from *July 25, 2015* to *September 6, 2015*.

Activities to be avoided when Venus is retrograde—

It's best not to take on any beautification projects (personal or otherwise) while Venus is retrograde. Try to avoid remodeling your home, getting a hair cut, perm, color, or changing your hair style. Especially avoid going to a new beautician. Also avoid cosmetic surgery. You won't be happy with the results of any of these activities when Venus is retrograde.

You will want to avoid major expensive purchases while Venus is Rx (retrograde). You won't be happy with them. It's a great time to shop at the flea markets, thrift stores and garage sales.

FIRST IMPRESSIONS ARE LASTING, AND SOMETIMES NOT ...

There are many things to consider when entering into a new, exciting and fresh relationship. The time that you meet someone can play a role in the rise and/or fall of a relationship. For example if you happen to meet your new love interest during a balsamic Moon, which is the twenty-four-hour period prior to the New Moon, the chances of a long and enduring relationship are slim. A meeting on or a few days following a New Moon is more likely to turn into an aspiring, budding relationship.

If you meet someone when the Moon is traveling through the sign of Scorpio or Taurus, sex may very well turn out to be a high priority in the relationship.

Timing is certainly a major factor to consider when you do meet someone. You've heard the saying, "right person, wrong time," or what can be even worse, "wrong person, right time." Sometimes we are just ready to meet someone—anyone—when the biggest mismatch of the century comes along and we don't even realize it. Or you meet the most wonderful person in the word and you're totally not available. Your head may not be in the right place for a relationship or you may already be in a committed relationship.

I suppose that is why, in my experience, a great majority of people who seek an astrological consultation do so when they are going through a relationship crisis.

WHAT'S IN YOUR NATAL PROMISE?

A natal promise is the signature or pattern that is found in a person's natal astrology chart. I can recall Carol Rushman saying at one of my UAC lectures that if a person has been married three or four times, it's not going to take much for them to marry again. But if a person has never been married and they are in their forties, fifties or sixties, it's going to take a major transit for them to marry.

What is it in our personalities that triggers or doesn't trigger relationships? What type of people do we attract? Some people attract relationships more easily than others because that is what is important to them, while others get a panic attack at the thought of having to deal with a relationship. This is all mapped out in your astrology chart for you as your natal promise. But remember, the stars impel, they don't compel. You always have free will to make your own decisions, even if you don't use it. But it stands to reason that it is an advantage to know the direction in which the stars impel you.

LOVE AND SECURITY

What do you want in a relationship? What satisfies

your sense of security? Why do some people keep going from one relationship to another with out finding fulfillment? What *is* fulfillment in a relationship? It's not an easy question. Is it love, security or both?

How do we find the love and security that we are looking for? For some people it comes many times in their life. For others it may come once in a lifetime. Once we find it, how do we keep or maintain it? All of these answers can be found in the stars. They can be found in your personal astrology chart.

Often times we say one thing but feel differently down deep inside. So we are not really attracting what we think we want. I remember years ago when I was single and had been for many years, I thought I wanted to get married and settle down, but I kept attracting the wrong kind of men—men who were unavailable. Something always blocked the way. They were either emotionally unavailable or they lived thousands of miles away from me. They weren't going to move and I wasn't going to move. Well, it just so happens that I have my Venus in Aquarius, which is not conducive or supportive of a person who really wants to settle down. There was a definite struggle going on between what I thought I wanted and what I really wanted.

The sign that Venus is in represents our expectations about love and companionship and what our true needs are. Aquarius represents space and freedom and independence. So as you can see I was dealing with mixed messages. I eventually learned how to integrate the dichotomy, but only after many heartbreaks and disappointments.

One heartbreaker who comes to mind was a friend from several years ago. He was studying Shamanism and developing his spiritual growth when we met at a metaphysical conference. He had worked for NASA during the Lunar Landing and I had worked for Grumman during the same period of time, so we had a lot in common. He was a Taurus Sun and Virgo Moon, which means he was very left brain. He was very analytical and practical, so I found it very unusual for him to be interested in metaphysical studies.

Because I have a Taurus Moon, there was a strong friendship and attraction between us, but his Virgo Moon was too analytical for me to deal with on a full-time basis. Although we lived two thousand miles apart, we stayed in touch for many years until we finally both met and married someone else.

Another former romantic possibility was fifty years old when we first met. He had never been married. I found it to be very interesting and a great case study when at age sixty he married for the first time. It was no surprise when I looked at his chart and saw that he was experiencing his second Saturn return.

Saturn had traveled back for the second time to the same sign and degree it was in when he was born. This takes place when a person is between fifty-eight and six-ty years old. This is one of the most important and major cycles in a person's life. Since it is approximately a twenty-nine-year cycle, the first Saturn return occurs when we are between twenty-eight and thirty years old.

This is generally when we take on major responsibili-ties, like getting married, having a baby, or buying our first home. It is often the time when we decide what we want to do when we grow up.

I guess my friend didn't grow up until his second Saturn return.

MARS/VENUS: PASSION OR LOVE?

When Mars hooks up with Venus, it can hit you like an overwhelming, out of control desire for passion and physical satisfaction. This occurs approximately every two years in the cycle of your life. It can be exciting, dangerous, thrilling and all-consuming. If you are in a committed relationship and your partner is ready, willing and able, this can be an exhilarating time. If you are not in a relationship there is a very good chance that you will attract someone to play out this theme.

I can recall one client who had recently gone through a divorce and after a long dry spell he decided to blow off some steam in Las Vegas. As they say, "what happens in Vegas stays in Vegas," so I won't go into all the details, except to say that as he was planning his trip I happened to notice that transiting Mars was coming up to join his natal Venus. When he returned, he shared with me that he had met a nurse at the poker table one night. He smiled suggestively and said, "It was a great trip."

Just because Mars is affecting your Venus it doesn't mean you have to act on it. The nice thing about understanding this astrological cycle is that you can work with it and, in some cases, keep yourself from getting into trouble. Or you can throw caution to the wind and go where it takes you.

Mary, a very lovely woman, came to me several years ago concerning relationship challenges she was experiencing. Her natal Venus was a high profile in her chart. Every time Mars came along and activated her Venus she would take advantage of the opportunities that came along with it. After she married, she was still attracted to other men when this cycle occurred. But fortunately, she realized that it was only a passing cycle and certainly not worth changing or ruining her marriage over. Planetary cycles come and go, but we always have control over how we respond to them. The stars impel; they don't control us.

Some people are born with Mars and Venus strongly connected. For them it can be a constant struggle to balance passion, love and sex in their life. It's not an easy signature to have in your natal birth chart, but understanding it and knowing about it can make it so much easier to deal with. For them life can be a journey of passionate turmoil or sexual bliss.

UNEXPECTED MATCHMAKER

One of the most popular questions I am asked during an astrology consultation is "when am I going to meet someone?" I remember a session with Susan, a client who was coming into a very positive relationship cycle. Her husband had passed away a couple of years prior and she was feeling that she was ready to meet someone. I confirmed that her chart was certainly supporting that feeling and manifestation. Transiting Jupiter, which means where Jupiter is traveling in the sky at the present time, was coming up to her natal Venus, meaning where Venus was at the time of her birth.

She explained that she lived in a small town which consisted mostly of retired people. She couldn't imagine where she was going to meet someone. But she also felt the time was right. I explained to her that timing is everything and it really doesn't matter where you live or what you do. When the time is right it just happens. I shared the following story with her.

A couple of years after my husband passed away I was driving by a local fruit market and decided on an impulse to stop and check out the produce. This was a place that I frequented but only occasionally. I wasn't what you would call a regular. I did not go every week on a certain day. It was a very random hit or miss type of thing.

On this particular day I happened to run into Dwain. Dwain was a heart transplant patient who was our campaign chairman when I worked at the American Heart Association. I hadn't seen him since my husband Larry had passed away. My late husband had also been a volunteer at the Heart Association, which is how they had known each other. He asked me how I was doing and if I was dating anyone.

He said that he had a friend who he thought I might enjoy meeting, and asked if I might be interested. Since he had known my late husband I figured he would know the type of man that I might be interested in, so I said sure. I gave him my card to pass on to his friend.

Several months went by and I totally forgot about my meeting with Dwain at the fruit market. Then one day out of the blue, the guy calls me and says, "Hi, I'm Tony, Dwain's friend." We chatted for a few minutes and he invited me to meet him for lunch at the beach where he was vacationing. There were only two things wrong with this. "The beach" happened to be sixty miles away. There was no way I was going to drive sixty miles to meet some guy that I didn't even know. And besides, it was the weekend that my son was coming home from college.

A couple of weeks later Tony called back and invited me to meet him for a drink after work. This time he was not sixty miles away. I arrived at the restaurant first and ran into some friends I hadn't seen in a while. They were seated at a window table, so I joined them while I waited for my blind date.

I'll never forget when I first laid eyes on him as he

was getting out of his car and walking across the parking lot. My friends immediately commented on how much he looked like my late husband. I couldn't believe my eyes. He was the same height and same build, and had similar mannerisms. Only when I looked into his eyes did I see a difference. They were blue and Larry's were brown.

Needless to say, drinks turned into dinner and dinner turned into many more dates, which eventually evolved into us getting married.

What was going on in our astrology charts at the time? Jupiter, the benefic guardian angel and planet that is credited for optimism and expansion, was just entering my 5th house of romance and wanting to have fun. It had been two years since my husband Larry had passed away and I was beginning to feel that I was ready for romance again. Jupiter was also "trining" my Sun, which means making a very good connection with my Sun at the time. I was well aware that good things can happen with this planetary connection.

With this in mind I had scheduled our blind date so we would meet on a New Moon. Naturally, I was not shy about asking Tony for his birth date. I was pleasantly surprised when I discovered that Jupiter was also making a very nice connection with his Sun sign and we had several favorable planetary connections in our charts.

This was to be a very fortuitous time for him as well. At least that was my desire and interpretation of our meeting. I pretty much expected this blind date to have a long term potential.

It so happened that my client Susan was also coming into a similar cycle when she came to see me. I was enthusiastic and encouraging, and she was very open to enjoying the romantic cycle which was beginning for her.

She had not met anyone since her husband had passed away—also about two years prior. As it turned out, she did meet a serious love interest a few months after our appointment.

"You must love yourself before you love another. By accepting yourself and joyfully being what you are, you fulfill your own abilities, and your simple presence can make others happy. "

~ Jane Roberts, *The Nature of Personal Reality*

CHAPTER TWELVE

FRIENDS AND FAMILY

CONNECTIONS THAT LAST A LIFETIME

In one of the first chapters of this book I admitted that the farther I traveled with astrology the more I saw how much farther I still had to go. There are so many aspects to this science and it isn't my expectation that anyone will remember all the connections—Sun/Jupiter and all the rest—which I've described while telling real life stories. Relax, there won't be a test. But I do hope you will have noticed that planetary connections are a key ingredient in relationships—be they romantic, family, friends or business. Some people call it chemistry. Whatever you call it, I can assure you that it can be seen in your astrological chart.

Have you ever wondered why some people come into

your life and they stay forever, while others are just brief acquaintances? It's all in the stars. When you have a planetary connection with someone, which means that one or more of your planets are in the same Sun sign as another person's planet or planets, this is called a planetary connection. And it is important.

There are many things in astrology that never cease to amaze me. One that makes me smile is working with the astrology charts of members of the same family. There are always strong connections between the parents and children. The interesting thing is that it does not have to be a biological relationship. I've seen this to be the case even when children were adopted.

CONNECTIONS

A planetary connection occurs when one or more planets in your chart are in the same sign and degree as one or more planets in another person's chart. They can come in all forms and sizes. They can be supportive, romantic, enduring, challenging, surprising, comforting or exasperating.

Since Saturn is the tester and teacher, when you have a Saturn connection with someone it usually indicates that there is work to be done with that person. And it is not usually fun. It is the kind of thing that you can't run away from or ignore. It's Karmic. It is meant to be. My late husband and I had a Saturn/Venus connection. This is often found when there is a significant age difference, which there was. He was fourteen years my senior and suffered with congestive heart failure for several years. Since I totally understood our connection and my roll, it was very natural for me to take care of him when his condition became chronic. Saturn is responsibility and Venus is love.

This can be the epitome of a Saturn/Venus connection. It certainly turned out that way in our case.

One of the most beautiful connections two people can have—and I often see this with parents and children—is the Sun/Moon connection.

After a long and stressful pregnancy and many natural child birth classes, my niece was informed at her pre-delivery checkup that the baby was breach. Her due date was May 11th and this was only April 18th. This baby had made her presence known almost from the moment of conception. There was the morning sickness, the afternoon sickness and the evening sickness, and then to find out that she was breach with no chance of having a natural child birth . . . Jolea was mortified when she was faced with having a cesarean section.

When I learned that the baby was due on May 11th I started running astrology charts in anticipation of what my great-niece would be like. What type of temperament would she have? In addition to her Taurus Sun, what sign would her Moon, Venus, Mercury and other planets be in? Since all of the planets play a role in a person's disposition and characteristics, I had already begun to imagine my great-niece's nature, and what she would look like. But this May 11th delivery date just didn't seem to fit her family profile.

It has been my experience that many children have a Sun/Moon connection with one or both or their parents, or some other strong planetary connection with one or both of their parents. On May 11th the Sun would be in Taurus and the Moon in Virgo. That was all well and good since Jolea's husband is a Taurus, but there was no planetary connection to the mother on this day. So I wasn't convinced that this was going to be her delivery date.

I said before that even when children are adopted they usually have a planetary connection with one or both of their adopted parents. It can even be true with step-parents. It is truly a beautiful thing to see because there is a strong bonding when this occurs. They feel very comfortable with each other, and very loved. I wanted this for my niece and her baby.

On April 25, my niece gave birth to a beautiful, healthy seven-pound, two-ounce baby girl with her Sun in Taurus—the same as her Daddy's Sun sign—and her Moon in Aquarius, the sign that her mother's Sun is in. This was the end of a very uncomfortable pregnancy, but it was the beginning of a beautiful and loving family. Whenever I see this planetary connection in a family chart or in a relationship chart I get a warm feeling. It is such a blessing to see a truly comfortable and loving connection.

> "AT THE MOMENT HE WAS BORN, HIS SUN WAS EXACTLY CONJUNCT WITH MY VENUS, WHICH REPRESENTS LOVE AND AFFECTION. I WAS SO EXCITED I COULD HARDLY STAND IT."

Yes, it does lift my spirits when I am working with a family and see this beautiful connection, but it's especially true when it is in my family. Is there any higher point in a life than the birth of a child? Well, the birth of grandchild runs a close second! The anticipation of my grandson's birth was very exciting as the family gathered in the hospital waiting area. My eyes remained glued to the clock so that I could personally record the moment he entered the world. Of course, since my son was in the delivery room, he also had instructions to be mindful of the exact time of his son's birth.

After holding the newborn and congratulating the

parents, my next immediate step was to get back to my computer and run the chart for my very special, wonderful grandson. I was certain that I was the only grandmother who had ever felt this way about her new grandchild. Since I had already consulted my astrological calendar before leaving for the hospital, I had a pretty good idea of what his chart was going to look like and what my relationship with him was going to be.

But it was even more special and exciting than I could have anticipated. At the moment he was born, his Sun was exactly conjunct with, also known as "together with" or "in the same degree as" my Venus, which represents love and affection. I was so excited I could hardly stand it.

Then, it got better. His Venus was conjunct with my Sun. Wow, that was a gift from heaven! I knew at that moment that this little boy and I were always going to be very close. My heart melted. I knew that he would be near and dear to my heart forever. As I have watched him mature and grow, our special connection has also grown.

A Venus/Sun connection is one of the most loving and beautiful connections that you can have with another person, and when it is reinforced in both charts that is really special.

Another family which comes to mind is a couple with two young boys. One of the boys has an Aquarius Moon which is in the same sign as his father's Sun sign, and the other has a Scorpio Moon which is in the same sign as his mother's Sun sign. When the children were not in the room I asked the mother if she felt a special closeness to one or the other of her children. She immediately referred to the child whose Moon is connected to her Sun. She further volunteered that her husband was closer to the child whose Moon was connected to his Sun. There seems to be an unexplainable bond between two people who have a Sun/Moon connection, especially when it is a parental bond.

I always love it when a client comes for a relationship compatibility or family dynamics consultation and I see this connection in their charts. Unless there is something else present in the chart that is creating a very contradictory and difficult aspect, a Sun/Moon or Venus/Sun conjunction can be a bonding and loving connection for life.

*"If you press me to say why I loved him, I can say
no more than because he was he, and I was I."*
~ Michel de Montalgne

CHAPTER THIRTEEN

WHEN LOVE IS IN THE STARS

FROM THE FAR SIDE OF THE WORLD

*When and where will you meet Mr. or Ms. Right? Timing is
everything and distance means nothing. It's all in the stars.*

After going to my favorite nail salon for several
years, which is owned and operated by the most
proficient and conscientious woman that I have ever met,
I *happened* to ask her one day how she met her husband.
Although I refer to her as a woman, she is younger than
my son so she seems more like a young girl to me. She is
without a doubt the hardest working young girl that I have
ever known—and totally devoted to her business and customers. And she gives the best manicure and pedicure
that I have ever experienced. And one more very important thing—cleanliness is next to Godliness in her salon.
You could eat off the floor and make chicken soup in her

pedicure foot baths. It's true, but I admit that it's not a very appetizing thought.

Although she is a Libra Sun sign, she has a strong Virgo presence in her chart. You never have to worry about getting a nail fungus when she does your pedicure. Her foot massages are to die for. As you probably can tell, I am one of her biggest fans. But then all of her customers love her.

She was born in Vietnam on the other side of the world from where I met her in Florida. She was well educated and came from an upper class family with one brother and four sisters. She enjoyed a close and happy family life and was brought up with exceedingly high work ethics and moral standards.

He lived in Daytona Beach and worked there as well. They were born and raised eleven thousand miles apart from each other. Neither of them had any idea that the other existed.

Then through a sheer stroke of luck—or was it luck?—one of his co-workers who happens to be from Vietnam mentioned that she had a very good friend whom she thought he would enjoy meeting. I know this sounds crazy but it's true.

With the help of the internet and cell phones they quickly became acquainted. The more he learned about her, the more interested and intrigued he became. He was fascinated with this intelligent and interesting woman from this far away land. As they got to know each other through the internet and phone conversations he soon realized that he had to meet her.

After several months of daily phone calls and emails,

> "ONE OF THE GREAT THINGS ABOUT BEING AN ASTROLOGY COUNSELOR IS THAT YOU GET TO BE PART OF REAL LIFE STORIES THAT WOULD BE IMPOSSIBLE TO DREAM UP."

they decided it was time to meet. So Phil, with great antici-pation, made the thirty-hour journey to Vietnam. Needless to say, neither of them was disappointed. He loved the country, he loved the food, he loved her family and most of all he loved her. Oh, did I mention that the lunar eclipse that year was in Libra making a very nice connection to both Hang and Phil's Sun? The handwriting was on the wall, or I should I say in the stars. This eclipse was an indi-cation that their lives were about to change over the next year. There were other visible astrological connections which helped this budding romance, but for now I'm go-ing to ask you to take my word for it. Right now I just want you to enjoy a love story.

During the course of two and a half years Phil made two more trips to Vietnam to see his special lady. Yes she found her tall, blond, handsome suitor to be very interest-ing and engaging as well. She was surprised at how easily he integrated himself into her world. After three visits of meeting the family and enjoying and appreciating her na-tive land, it was decision time. Remember, she's a Libra and does not make decisions quickly.

Finally, when the lunar eclipse took place on Hang's Mars, the planet of action, she did move from Vietnam to the United States. She was taken away from her homeland and transplanted to a new environment and culture. But it didn't seem to bother her for a second. She quickly ob-tained her nail technician license and started working in a salon. This was before she opened her own salon. Since she is a Libra Sun sign with many other planets in Libra, she was not going to jump into marriage too quickly. She knew that once she made a commitment it was going to be permanent. So there was no rush. She adjusted to living and working in the United Sates while she continued with getting to know her suitor better.

Naturally, after hearing this incredible story about how these two unlikely people met when they lived half a world apart, I couldn't wait to get home and calculate their astrology charts. I also calculated the charts for the time that Phil first contacted her, the first time he flew to Vietnam to meet her and, of course, their wedding date.

It was all so very fascinating and it once again proved to me that the stars most definitely do have an influence on our lives, even when we don't realize it or consciously do anything to help the stars along.

HOW THEY MATCHED UP ASTROLOGICALLY

Hang has her Sun, Moon, Mercury, and Pluto in Libra. Phil's Sun and Mercury are in Aquarius. As you may recall, these are all air signs which would give them a strong attraction or compatibility right off the bat. If they were at a party with a hundred other people they would find each other. They would be like magnets that would attract each other.

Here's where the good stuff comes in—the romance. Phil's natal Venus, the planet of love and romance, makes a very nice connection to Hang's natal Sun. His Jupiter, the guardian angel, also favorably connects with her Sun. So not only do they have a strong communication between them, there is also a strong romantic attraction. Both are very positive connections to have in a relationship.

I would like to be able to say that some Vietnamese or American astrologer brought them together, but that wasn't the case. Their love affair was something that was just meant to be.

The Vietnamese friend of Hang's who vicariously introduced them was a Taurus Sun sign, which is the same sign that Phil's Saturn is in. Her Saturn also made a very nice connection with Hang's Saturn. Both of these connections with their mutual friend indicate a strong and enduring friendship. She is someone who would want to look after both of them and be very sincere in her efforts. They all continue to remain friends.

THE WEDDING

One of the great things about being an astrology counselor is that you get to be part of real life stories that would be impossible to dream up. And my favorite stories are the love stories. Hang had been living in the United States for another fifteen months before she accepted Phil's proposal. As I stated before, she is a Libra Sun sign and has to think about things for quite a while before she makes a decision. But when transiting Jupiter, the guardian angel, came up to her natal Venus, the planet of love, she was ready to make the lifelong commitment. I must say I couldn't have selected a better wedding date for them if I had picked it myself.

This just goes to prove once again that the planets do affect us, even when we don't pay any attention to them. Some people like me are called to understand how they affect us and to share that information with others on a daily basis.

For those of you who are familiar with the astrological language, you will appreciate that this is a textbook example of the planets in action. But whether you are a curious novice or a longtime follower of astrology, you'll appreciate that I knew intuitively from the beginning that something more than dumb luck had to be at work to bring two people together from opposite sides of the world.

And, if you've been reading carefully, you'll also appreciate that just because they were married on an auspicious day when the planets were lined up nicely for them—and their astrology charts show a lot of nice connections—it doesn't mean that their life together is always going to be perfect. Every couple, no matter how perfectly compatible they are, can expect to have some challenges in their marriage or they wouldn't be human.

*"If you're in a bad situation, don't worry it'll change.
If you're in a good situation, don't worry it'll change."*

~ John A. Simone Sr.

CHAPTER FOURTEEN

URANUS THE WORLD ROCKER

HOLD ON TIGHT!

Uranus, the bearer of unexpected events, can surprise you like a bolt of lightning on a sunny day. It can come totally out of the blue and change your life. Whatever area of your chart that it is affecting can totally rock your world and turn your life up side down.

FRED'S STORY

It was very late one night when I received a phone call from my friend, Fred. I could tell by his voice that he was very shaken and upset. His father had passed away two weeks prior and he had just received a phone call telling him that his step-mother had been killed in an automobile accident. Since he was the only child, duty and emotions prevailed. He immediately made arrangements to fly cross country the next morning. The responsibility for making funeral arrangements and sorting out the estate would fall on him and him alone.

His life would certainly be rocked and turned upside down. The fortunate thing he had going for him was that he was born with Saturn and his Sun connected. This means that it is his nature to be a grounded and serious person. He takes duties and responsibilities very seriously. There was no question in his mind that he would do whatever needed to be done when he arrived in Oregon.

Since the Sun represents the essence of who you are, and Saturn represents your duties, responsibilities and lessons in life, this was certainly a calling he was very qualified to handle.

When someone dies unexpectedly two weeks after their spouse it can be a real rat's nest trying to figure out the estate—especially if the paperwork is not in order. Many times people just bounce through the days, feeling that there is always plenty of time in the future to make changes to the will or to organize all of life's many documents—financial and otherwise. But when there is a sudden, unexpected accident everything changes. It is left to the surviving family members to sort through the paperwork.

In this case Fred was the only surviving family member so he was left with the overwhelming task. As I quickly ran his chart, it was very obvious that transiting Uranus was sitting on his ascendant, indicating unexpected life-changing events would occur. Uranus also happened to be opposing the ruler of his 8th house, which is the house that rules inheritances.

My experience has been that any time Uranus is involved with a person's 8th house, there is an unexpected inheritance. The accidental death of Fred's step-mother certainly could not have been more of a surprise. He had just spoken with her the night before the accident. She was in excellent health. She was planning to sell the house after she finished up all of the business she needed to handle after losing her husband.

Although I would never try to advise a client as to the timing of a death, the timing of an inheritance can often times be very apparent in a person's chart.

The fact that Uranus was sitting on his ascendant made this event even more dramatic for him. After studying his chart I realized that this would be a life-altering event for him. Fred's life would change forever.

> "THIS WAS A PERFECT EXAMPLE OF URANUS IN ACTION, THE PLANET THAT BRINGS SURPRISES WHEN YOU LEAST EXPECT THEM."

The 1st house, which is where the ascendant is located in a natal chart, represents your physical body and how you are perceived by the world. It describes your personality, appearance, disposition and outlook on life. As Isabel Hickey wrote in *Astrology a Cosmic Science*, your ascendant or 1st house is "the window to the world." As he looked out that window, he now saw the world with a whole new perspective. His inheritance would certainly change his outlook.

ESTELLE'S STORY

Estelle was adopted when she was four years old and never knew her biological father. You can imagine her shock one day when she received a phone call out of the blue from a "people finder." It seems that there are companies that specialize in finding missing or lost heirs. They receive a percentage of the estate settlement for their trouble. One of these companies had searched for and found her, overcoming the fact that she was living three thousand miles away from her deceased biological father. Her mother had remarried when she was a young child and her new husband quickly adopted Estelle. Even though Estelle had been married three times, it seems that in this day of the internet and computer databases there is no hiding from your past.

Fortunately, her biological father was living in California at the time of his death. It seems that according to California law, adoption does not preclude an inheritance from your biological parents. Since her father had no other children, she was the legal heir to his estate.

Estelle had inherited her father's estate when transiting Uranus entered her 8th house. At the time of this unexpected windfall, Uranus also happened to be traveling over her natal Mercury, which is the ruler of her 2nd house. The 2nd house represents personal finances. This was truly written in the stars.

This was a perfect example of Uranus in action, the planet that brings surprises when you least expect them. The curious thing about all this is that Estelle, responding to an unexplained urge or intuition, had been trying to locate her biological father several months earlier, which was about the same time that he passed away.

PART III

A STEADY BREEZE

SAILING ON LIFE'S SEA

"HAPPINESS IS FOUND ALONG THE WAY,
NOT AT THE END OF THE ROAD."
~ AUTHOR UNKNOWN

"Life is full and overflowing with the new.
But it is necessary to empty out the old
to make room for the new to enter."

Eileen Caddy, **Footprints on the Path**

CHAPTER FIFTEEN
MERCURY RETROGRADE
HANDLE WITH CARE

It always amazes me when people who know nothing about astrology all of a sudden become very interested as soon as the subject of Mercury retrograde arises—especially when it *is* retrograde. Everyone living on this planet can relate to this cycle. Even the media has mentioned it. I can recall watching CNBC when they were interviewing Arch Crawford, a well known financial astrologer. He was discussing how Mercury being retrograde affects the stock market.

I would feel remiss if I did not include a chapter about Mercury, the planet that rules communications, computers, telephones, travel and anything that is a communications or connection device.

Mercury is considered one of the "personal planets" because it travels in close relationship to planet Earth. We feel its effects more personally than we do the outer planets—Uranus, Pluto and Neptune. Since Mercury is so up close and personal, we can relate to it on a daily basis, especially when it is traveling in retrograde motion.

Mercury goes retrograde approximately three times a year for twenty-one days. When Mercury is retrograde it means that it is moving in an apparent backward motion. This can affect all areas of communication and travel. Appointments will typically have to be rescheduled or will run late. Documents can be lost or misplaced. Faulty machinery can become an issue. Promises are often broken and information can be misleading and unclear. Repairs are often needed on computers and automobiles when Mercury is retrograde.

> I ACTUALLY LOOK FORWARD TO THESE PERIODS AND SAVE APPROPRIATE PROJECTS FOR THEM. IT IS A TIME TO PLAY CATCH UP.

This is typically not a good time to negotiate or sign new contracts. But if you must, make certain that you have read and re-read all of the details and small print. Do not leave anything to chance. Telephones, computers and other related sources of communication could malfunction unexpectedly.

Some of the ways you can work with this cycle is to avoid shopping or making major purchases such as a new automobile or a computer. On the other hand, purchasing a used automobile is not as troublesome when Mercury is retrograde. I can recall purchasing a new automobile during this cycle that turned out to be a lemon. I took the car back to the dealer several times because the steering was loose. They kept trying without success to figure out what the problem was. Unfortunately, I ended up having to trade my car after Mercury went direct. And no, the dealer did not acknowledge that it was a lemon.

Because computers and all electronic communications devices can be so strongly affected by the Mercury retrograde cycle, you can be assured that any needed repairs that you have been putting off will come to the surface.

AIR TRAVEL WITH MERCURY RX

Thinking of taking a trip? You may want to make sure that Mercury is not retrograde before planning your dream vacation. It has been my experience that there are more delays and mixed up reservations during this cycle. There is a greater likelihood that your luggage will be lost. If you must travel, check and recheck your reservations. Don't leave anything to chance. Traveling to a location you have visited before does not seem to be as troublesome as new locations can be.

Since a picture is worth a thousand words, this is one example of a Mercury Rx vacation that is a classic. I can still vividly recall our family's Mercury retrograde ski trip from several years ago. We flew into the "old" Denver Airport on the last day that was in operation.

The home scene at our hotel was crazy on the morning of our departure. After getting up in the middle of the night to make the long drive to the airport for what we thought was a very early flight, we learned upon arrival at the airport that we were actually there four hours early. It seems that we had misread the itinerary.

We were flying out of the "new" airport, which none of us were familiar with, so we dropped my son and daughter-in-law off at the check-in curb with all of our suitcases, skis and ski boots. My husband and I then proceeded to return the rental car, which required driving to a separate building away from the main terminal. We agreed to meet in the atrium. When we returned on the rent-a-car shuttle we didn't realize that there were duplicate atriums. We each thought we were in the right place. This of course was in the days before cell phones were so pervasive.

This is a perfect example of the kind of miscommunication that can take place—the Mercury retrograde effect at its fullest. Emotions and tempers were running a little hot since we had all spent so much time waiting at our wrong locations that we almost missed our flight. Fortunately this was before 9/11 and we didn't have to go through the security check. Since it cost us nothing more than a little anxiety, it ended up in retrospect being a good family story. But it wasn't so funny at the time.

MORE TRAVELS, MORE MERCURY RX ADVENTURES

A week after the infamous hurricane Charley hit our home town in Florida in 2004, we left on a pre-scheduled vacation to Las Vegas. Little did we know that we would be cutting our trip short so that we could return home before they closed the Orlando airport. It seemed that hurricane Frances was heading our way.

I certainly know better than to go on vacation when Mercury is retrograde because communications and instructions between everyone involved can become confused. However, this happened to be the week that our timeshare was available so we really didn't have a choice. I would not have been surprised if our flight had been delayed since that is another common occurrence when Mercury is retrograde. And I always take a carry-on with overnight essentials and medication.

By now you may think I'm saying you should crawl

under a rock or into a hole to hibernate when Me
retrograde. That may not be a bad idea, but this a
be a very productive time. It is a wonderful oppc
and very auspicious time for you to re-group, re-organize,
re-read, and re-think your decisions. You can use this time
to re-write and re-process information. Think of this time
as a dark of the Moon or balsamic Moon cycle that lasts for
twenty-one days. The balsamic Moon is the twenty-four-
hour period before the New Moon when the Moon shows
no light (*to review the Moon phases see page 62-64*).

I actually look forward to these periods and save appropriate projects for them. It is a time to play catch up.
This is when you can clean out your closets and drawers. If
you are a pack rat you will be surprised at how motivated
you can become during this cycle.

A ROAD TRIP WITH MERCURY RX

We checked the weather before beginning our road
trip to northern Georgia and Tennessee where we planned
to visit friends and family and play golf. We knew it had
been raining, but the forecast was predicted to improve in
a couple of days. After spending the night in Atlanta, we
checked the weather forecast again and saw that there was
flooding to the west and north of us. Several of the major
interstates had been closed. Fortunately our escape route
to the south was still open. So, with great disappointment,
we ended our trip in Atlanta and headed back home.

I knew that Mercury is the ruler of travel, travel planning and our mental processing, so I was not surprised
by this forced change of plans. In retrospect, we probably should have called the trip off in the first place.
Poor thinking and judgment on our part, but who would
have guessed that Georgia would have its worst deluge

of rain in over one hundred years.

I was well aware that Mercury was going to be retrograde when we scheduled the trip, so I checked and doubled-checked all of our reservations. Everything was in order except the weather. Knowing what I know may have fooled me into thinking I could control the situation with careful attention to detail. But doubts about the weather were riding with us from the time we left home. Despite all I did to make sure everything would go smoothly, natural forces beyond my control were at work. I can say that understanding these natural forces did help me to go with the flow and not get upset.

PRODUCTIVE MERCURY RETROGRADE IN ACTION

If showing it is better than explaining it, real-life stories about Mercury retrograde experiences have got to be worth something. Each month I publish an astrology newsletter on my website where I highlight what is going on for the month. It is especially interesting when there is a Mercury retrograde cycle to write about. The following is some of the feedback that I have received from my clients over the years:

> *"Well THAT certainly explains my unplanned cleaning frenzy. I began with my closet. Only took eleven hours ... If what I discarded from my closet is any reflection of what I must "discard" from other areas of my life — it will be a very interesting and maybe a long 21 days! Thanks for the heads up, Kelly!" Jackie P.*

> *"I had my first garage sale this weekend and it was a great success. Feels so good to let go of items that no longer serve my highest and best! It helped to work*

with the Mercury Rx energy" Thanks Kelly

"This retrograde cycle we took advantage of the clearing energy and cleaned out our entire garage, attic, closets, drawers, laundry room, and rearranged our kitchen counter-top to be more organized. It seemed so easy to let go of things during this cycle, in fact I felt a 'push' to do so. It was time to let go of all of our baby items and boy did we let go! Everything is now gone from the house and I had arranged for it to be shared with a few different charity organizations, a consignment store, as well as a cousin who is pregnant. I had the energy to actually clear things out, pack them up, AND take or ship them to the appropriate place rather than let them sit around the house for months before I would get around to it. We got organized, cleared out, and made way for new things. Now I am ready to take a look at the next phase of life with room for new 'stuff' and opportunities to come."

"Retrograde cycles are a great time to send the kids to Grandma's house. We realized that the last time our son spent time with Grandma and Grandpa was during the last Mercury retrograde cycle (the last time we went through the garage!)." Wendy Hamrick

"It was helpful to know that it was coming and when it ended, as that motivated me to finish or complete what I had to do with regards to clearing stuff out by a certain time. I will definitely use this to my advantage in the future! Thanks Kelly." As always "G"

"This is great . . . I needed this right now . . . I cleaned out a bunch today with the girl that cleans for me . . . now I will do more . . . maybe the garage, but its too hot. I think there is still plenty left to be uncluttered . . . thank you so much. I really needed to hear about what was going on with Mercury."

◯　◯　◯

"I have been having a good time cleaning out and reorganizing my closets and garage. As luck would have it, the school at my church is having a rummage sale at the end of this month, so I have been motivated to recycle some of my treasures and make room for more."

MERCURY RX AND ELECTRONICS

On a personal note, I happened to be in Radio Shack looking for a hands-free Bluetooth, the kind you put on the visor of your car. While I was there, the Sirius radio just happened to catch my eye. My husband has both of these very cool items in his car and I have been coveting them. My 2004 model is not equipped with either of these luxuries. So on a whim, knowing full well that Mercury was retrograde (not a good time to purchase electronics or phones) I decided to ignore my better judgment. Sometimes, I confess, I'm like many people: better at giving good advice than following it. But after all, I was already there in the store, and it was a whole lot cheaper than buying a new car. Patience has never been one of my virtues. Wait until Mercury went direct? No way was I going to do that.

You guessed it. I ended up going back to Radio Shack because I was having a problem with the Bluetooth. It did not seem to be compatible with my phone. It seemed to be having a hard time recognizing my iPhone. I figured that I might as well get the Sirius radio while I was there too. For reasons that are too long to explain, I ended up returning the radio. The general moral to this story is that you may not be satisfied with items that you purchase while Mercury is retrograde, particularly electronics. My personal moral was that being an astrology counselor doesn't put me beyond the influences of the planets. Nor does it privilege me to always use good judgment.

CHALLENGES WITH MERCURY RX

Forewarned is forearmed. If you understand and work with the Mercury retrograde cycles the bazaar things that happen can actually be funny. If you are not tuned in to what is going on, it can drive you crazy. These are some more examples shared by friends and clients.

> "It was really good to hear from you. I have been a bit concerned. When I didn't get the Newsletter this month, I emailed you; thought you might have had a family situation that kept you from sending it out. When I didn't get a response from the email, I tried to call you. The number I had has been disconnected and information could find nothing listed for you. Checked your Web Site for a number, computer message said Web Site cannot be located. Tried twice more, same thing happened. So Now I am really concerned so I googled you. Several links came up I clicked on one ... it was infected! I freaked and tried to cancel. Nothing happened so I called my computer tech friend, he told me I should have called him before I clicked cancel because that is the trick to spread the virus. I'm virus free now. Gave my computer to the tech. He ran scans and disconnected and reconnected all my protections. What an experience! I am always oh so cautious

about opening anything when I don't recognize the name. When I did get an email ('astrologytalk') from you I was afraid to open it. Called my tech, he told me to open it while he was on the phone ... all was well and I'm glad you are too! "

Betty Riley, Atlanta, Ga.

The other part of this Mercury Rx story, which makes it even more ironic is that this email went into my deleted file, unopened. I just happened to scan through that file before I was going to permanently delete it. I have never before or since had any friend or client report this experience. Here's more Mercury Rx trouble from clients, friends and colleagues—

"Last night I tried to pay a bill online and the bill pay server was down. Still is today."

○   ○   ○

"Just now, I tried to log into Microsoft money and it told me my password was no good. So I changed passwords. It will not take the new one either, and that server turns out to be down as well." Cyndy

○   ○   ○

"Bank of America's online Portfolio service which allows clients to track their transactions is on the fritz and has had 1000 calls this morning about it. Mercury again ..." Barbara Nelen, Orlando, FL

○   ○   ○

"I arrived for my four o'clock manicure appointment which I had made that morning, only to find out that the appointment was for 4:45. I had to laugh when I remembered that Mercury was Rx."

○   ○   ○

"Friggin Mercury Rx! Car runs great and all of a sudden—a dry bearing around the timing belt which was already replaced! GRRR!!!" Barbara Nelen, Orlando, FL

○ ○ ○

"I just had to smile. My son and daughter in-law and I have been counting and we are up to 15 Mercury retrograde happenings. All the way from electricity, coffee pots, cell phones, believe me a list of 15 so far. Ya just have to smile, it's kind of fun to blame it on something. Fortunately no disasters". Rollie Allen, Windermere, FL

○ ○ ○

"Hi Kelly! I was thinking of you lately . . . This Retrograde period really hit hard . . . My fiancé Mike is selling his house in Miami. He has a buyer and the closing was to take place 4/15, well it didn't . . . Now it's been extended until??? Today, we are still waiting. In the meantime I moved to Ga 3/25, and I'm waiting for Mike to come . . . but??? Also, my sister had major problems with her iPhone & computer. She's in the process of getting them fixed . . . When is the next one coming?? I think I'll go on vacation, lol . . . Thanks for the B-message. Take Care!"

○ ○ ○

"It seems that retail stores survive on discount coupons and special sales and they always do big promotions around the holidays to entice shoppers. It was the week before Easter and Mercury was Rx, although I knew it was not a good time to shop, the sales and coupons were too enticing to resist. Needless to say, I ended up having to return almost everything that I purchased."

A TRIP TO THE DENTIST WITH MERCURY RETROGRADE

On a personal note, I had the opportunity, or should I say misfortune, to experience Mercury retrograde in action at the dentist. It seems that no matter how hard we try to prepare and how aware we are of the influence that this cycle can have on us, it still finds its way into our lives. Several weeks prior to Mercury stationing Rx I had a root canal procedure. I didn't want to wait too long to have the crown prep work done and thereby take a chance of the tooth cracking.

Unfortunately, I had to schedule it during the retrograde period. As I'm sitting in the dental chair, prior to the injection, I ask half jokingly, "You are sure which tooth needs the crown?" So as not to sound insulting or doubting his work, I explained that Mercury was retrograde and what it meant. I explained that it would not be unusual for mistakes to be made or something to go wrong at this time.

As his office manager overheard this conversation, she said, "Well that explains what has been going on all week. This has been a horrendous week of emergencies and schedule changes." They both wanted to know how long this was going to last.

After the injection took effect, he came back into the room to begin the drilling, and guess what? The air compressor would not work. When I shared this story with my husband, who is a retired dentist, he said that in all of his thirty-seven years of practice, he never had that happen.

I learned later, after I made my sixty-mile trip back home, that it was just a speck of dust that had gotten into the compressor and caused it to shut down. They were able to fix it shortly after I left. His office manager said that she was really glad I had come in because it helped them understand what had been going on all week. It had been one crazy week.

Much to my surprise I didn't even get upset about the long drive and the wasted injection. And I am the biggest baby when it comes to those injections! I actually thought it was rather comical since I knew full well what was going on with the universe. Had I not known, I probably would not have taken it so well. Although we can't always control what happens to us, we can control how we respond. It has been my experience that astrology can be very helpful in this respect.

As I mentioned earlier, there is a productive and positive side to this Mercury Rx cycle. This is an excellent time to clean out you closets and drawers, or reorganize you home or office space. It also is the perfect time to rid yourself of old hurts and unkind memories you've harbored too long, and get ready for Mercury to go direct.

MERCURY RX AND ELECTIONS

I always find it interesting to watch the elections when they take place during a Mercury Rx. These are a few perfect examples of Mercury Rx in action:

The Florida recount in the presidential election of the year 2000 was a period of vote re-counting that occurred following the unclear results of the 2000 United States presidential election contest between George W. Bush and Al Gore. The Florida results were especially unclear. The election was ultimately settled in favor of George W. Bush when the U.S. Supreme Court, with its final ruling on Bush v. Gore, stopped a recount that had been proposed by the Florida Supreme Court, which had the effect of awarding Bush a majority of votes in the Electoral College. Most of us remember the absolute chaos of the entire process. Is it any surprise that this took place while Mercury was Rx?

INAUGURATION DAY

After **the public inauguration flub** that was heard around the world, President Barack Obama took the oath of office ... again! Chief Justice John Roberts delivered the oath to Mr. Obama on Wednesday night at the White House after the initial oath ceremony—a rare do-over.

The surprising makeup moment came in response to Tuesday's much-noticed stumble, when Roberts got the words of the oath a little off—which prompted President Obama to do so, too.

Don't worry, the White House said: Obama has still been president since noon on Inauguration Day.

Nevertheless, the Associated Press news service reported, Obama and Roberts went through the drill once again out of what White House counsel Greg Craig called "an abundance of caution."

Yes, you guessed it: Mercury was retrograde during this event.

I received this from a vigilant client regarding the January 2008 elections ...

"I am wondering if it is just me or if everyone is feeling the confusion and frustration about this election day? My husband and I tried to dissect the sample ballet while digesting our breakfast. My breakfast was more meaningful. We couldn't make heads or tails out of the 'Amendment 1' and the multitude of candidates made my head spin. If this isn't a perfect example of Mercury Retrograde I don't know what is. Isn't Mercury the planet that rules the way we think and process information? I guess when it's retrograde,

it does cause information to become tangled and con-
fused. This is the first time in my life that I can recall
being so undecided when I stood in the voting booth."

○ ○ ○

THE MERCURY RX TAKE-AWAY

Again I want to emphasize that although the Mercury Rx cycle can be challenging, it can also be a very freeing cycle and a time to discover some items that you forgot you owned because they have been buried in the back of a cabinet, pantry or drawer. This is an opportunity to think about the areas of your life you want to clean out and reorganize. After all, there is a lot to be said for simplicity. Remember, whenever we let something go, we make space for something new. This can be a very exhilarating and productive cycle. When Mercury goes direct it usually means that life will get back on track or back to normal. That which has been put on hold can materialize and move forward.

"Success is a journey not a destination—
half the fun is getting there."

~ Geta Bellin

CHAPTER SIXTEEN

SAILING AROUND THE WORLD

IGNORANCE ISN'T ALWAYS BLISS

In keeping with my lifelong dream of sailing around the world, I did have an opportunity to at least sail across the ocean. I was so exited when I learned I would finally fulfill at least a part of my dream.

I had taken a two-week vacation to help deliver a forty-five-foot sailing yacht to St. Maarten for a charter company. Since I had never been to the island, the trip was all about the adventure for me. The plan was to sail there and fly home. Two weeks would allow plenty of time to relax and enjoy St. Maarten before I had to return to work.

The day and time the captain chose for our departure was calculated based on the weather forecast and the tides. Everyone knows that the tides are directly affected by the Moon. Since this was my first big sailing adventure, my excitement was beyond words. As we set sail from Ft. Lauderdale it wasn't long before I noticed that the seas looked a whole lot bigger sitting in this little sailboat than they had seemed when I looked out on the ocean from the beach. And my stomach was not handling them well. Fortunately, I had brought along "the patch," which is a little band-aid that you put behind your ear to prevent sea sickness.

We were all elated as we set out on our journey to this far away island. But a big surprise was waiting in store for us. What we didn't know was that the connection between the battery and the engine was not working properly, so eventually the battery died and the engine quit working. This caused the lights, navigation system and refrigeration on the yacht to stop working as well. You might think that wouldn't matter on a sailboat, but unfortunately we were traveling due southeast, which is exactly where the wind was coming from. So we were motoring into the wind until our motor died. Then we were tacking back and forth into the wind, which makes it a much longer journey. It's always better to sail a direct course with the wind at your back. But as with life, this is seldom the case.

> "A LOT OF BOATS ARE LOST AT SEA. NOW I KNOW WHY!"

Fortunately, our captain was skilled in celestial navigation, which means he used a hand-held instrument called a sextant to navigate by the position of the Sun. This certainly took a lot more time than the sophisticated electronic device with which the yacht was equipped, but since we had no power, we had no choice.

The worst part of this was that our German cook had stocked our freezer with mostly meats and perishables.

Food would eventually become an issue if the wind di[d] co-operate with us and our journey was too prolonged.

But it got worse than spoiled knockwurst. One night I was assigned the 3 a.m. to 6 a.m. helm duty. Everyone was asleep below deck. At first it was grand. We were moving very nicely under full sail on a beautiful clear night. I had never seen so many stars. The sky is so different when you are out in the middle of the ocean and there are no distracting lights. Then, all of a sudden, out of literally nowhere this huge black cloud appeared and the wind picked up to at least fifty miles an hour. I started screaming for help from the rest of the crew that was sleeping below deck.

Fortunately, it was the Captain's policy that whenever you are on the helm at night—which means steering the boat at night—you had to wear a life line, which is a harness that is attached to a railing. This is to prevent being lost at sea in case you fall overboard. Now that's a comforting thought!

As the other four crew members came charging up to help, I ran up to the bow, the front of the boat, and started bringing down the sails. As I was holding on to whatever part of the boat I could grab, the wind and the waves almost washed me overboard. I saw water in the pitch dark of the night rushing up to my knees on the deck of the boat. My whole life flashed before me, seeing it all in a split second as others have said happens when death is threatening. I prayed to God that if I got off of this boat alive, I would *never* sail across the ocean again.

Fortunately, the wind subsided as the black cloud moved across the ocean almost as suddenly as it had appeared. Although it was a flash storm—it seems that is very common in the middle of ocean—the damage that it left behind added to our already handicapped situation.

ripped, which crippled our sailing ability.
ease our cruising speed even more. So
n the open sea, with no engine and only
il we could figure out a way to mend the
ntually did. We were not a pretty site. But
as lost at sea or injured.

On another night during this eventful sail to St. Maarten, while I was asleep below deck, I was awakened by loud noises on deck. The jib sail was flopping back and forth without a trace of wind in the air, which was making a heck of a noise.

As we all scrambled to the deck we saw a huge tanker heading right for us. Since we had no power we couldn't motor out of its way, and we had no lights so they didn't even see us. It seems that we had drifted into the shipping channel and could not get out of the tanker's way. I didn't realize it, but these tankers are set on automatic pilot and just charge through the shipping channel at full steam. A lot of boats are lost at sea. Now I know why!

Someone thought to grab a mirror and a flash light so we could make a reflection, since that was the only thing we could do. We were totally and helplessly adrift and could not move out of the tanker's path. We were caught in its crosshairs.

After what seemed like an eternity, the tanker moved off but still passed within less than half a football field from us. Believe me when I say that distance *feels* like mere inches when you are a little boat watching a humongous steel tanker approaching you. We were all well aware of the potential and very imminent life-threatening danger that we had escaped. Not only had we dodged a direct hit from the tanker, we could have been sucked into the ocean by the wake of this enormous steel monster in the pitch dark of night—never to be seen or heard from again. My parents would never have forgiven me.

Fifteen days after leaving port on what was supposed to be a seven-day sail to St. Maarten, our adventure came to what we thought was the end as we maneuvered our way through a dark and difficult harbor. Fortunately, our captain had plotted a course through this harbor before, because even in the light of day with a working engine it could be a challenge. And here we were attempting this at 2 a.m. under full sail! This was not an easy task. The adventure was not over yet. As tired and weary as we were, our hearts were still in our throats.

There were a lot of happy shouts and screams as the lines were thrown out and we finally settled in at the dock. The captain had a "no alcohol" rule on the trip. But when we docked in St. Maarten after our fifteen-day adventure, the captain broke open his bottle of rum. Believe me, we all needed it.

When we met the dock master the next morning, we learned that they were getting ready to send out the Coast Guard to search for us. The charter company was not very happy when they saw their weather-beaten and sail-tattered boat. But, hey, we arrived safe and sound.

Needless to say, that ended my desire to sail around the world. I decided to never again sail beyond sight of land.

I must confess that I was a novice student of astrology during this time in my life. I really had no earthly idea about the importance of timing and how important it is to select the right time to begin a trip—especially a trip of this significance. I also had no idea of the potential danger that could arise when you are at sea in a small boat. And, I might add, this was long before pirating had become so prevalent. This is one part of my life that I am happy to see in my rearview mirror, never to travel that road—or those seas—again. I don't even go on cruise ships.

"If you believe in forever then life is just a one night stand."
~ Everly Brothers

CHAPTER SEVENTEEN
BORN UNDER A LUCKY STAR?
THE ADVANTAGE OF FAVORABLE WINDS

He had finally reached the dream of his lifetime. He was going to Las Vegas to play in a World Championship Poker tournament. The entry fee was more then he had ever put up in a poker game in his life. So the winning stakes were equally as high. There were three thousand players who had signed up to play in this world event tournament. This was his dream come true.

When he arrived at the poker ballroom it was bigger and more overwhelming than he could have ever imagined. There were three hundred poker tables set up for the three thousand players. The tournament was to begin at noon. He could feel the lump in his throat as he tried to swallow. He could hardly believe that he was really there. He had seen this poker room on TV many times, but it was far bigger then he ever dreamed it would be. He had arrived.

He had aspired to play in this tournament ever since he started playing poker in college. He was actually a pretty good player. Of course, he had his ups and downs but for the most part he was way ahead. It wasn't about the money; it was more about the challenge of playing the game. He enjoyed the camaraderie of playing with his buddies. He was a social person and this was certainly a socially interactive game for him. He loved reading people and trying to figure them out. It was truly about playing the game.

"THE LESSON OF THIS STORY IS YOU DON'T HAVE TO KNOW ANYTHING ABOUT ASTROLOGY—OR EVEN BELIEVE IN IT—FOR IT TO WORK. IT HAS A SYSTEM AND ENERGY ALL ITS OWN. AND IT'S ALWAYS WORKING."

His intellectual, social Gemini Sun sign and his free-spirited, adventurous and optimistic Sagittarius Moon were very well suited for this momentous occasion. He had traveled thousands of miles to play with the big boys. And he was looking forward to every minute of it.

Once the game actually began, the marathon was on with only short intermittent breaks. Even though he was young and had prepared physically and mentally for this arduous tournament, it was beginning to takes its toll on him. He had to regroup and focus. But he was getting fairly good cards, good enough to stay afloat.

On the final day of the tournament he had a 10:45 p.m. reservation to fly home. Since he really didn't believe he would make it to the final table, he booked that flight time thinking it would give him ample opportunity to enjoy some leisure time after he was eliminated. But the stars had something else in mind for him. Little did he know that on this last day of the tournament his chart would be lit up like the Las Vegas strip at night.

I will go into greater detail in a moment, but at this time let me just say that this was indeed destined to be his lucky day.

No matter how great a poker player you are, luck still plays a big part in deciding whether you win or lose a hand—especially when playing against other skilled players. You can go "all in" with a pair of aces and someone may be holding a king and queen and they call you and draw two queens on the flop. Besides luck, you have to have patience. You need the patience to wait for the right hand. This was something that Huleo was very good at doing.

As he was immersed in playing at the final table—yes he made the final table—he began to realize that he had a plane to catch that evening and commitments back home the next day that could not be postponed.

He was feeling it in his bones. He had made the final table. Something big was about to happen. Not only was he getting great cards but he was the chip leader by more then double anyone else at the final table. There was only one small problem. He was running out of time. He began mentally counting down the time he had remaining to play. He still had that plane to catch, which was the last plane of the day out of Las Vegas that could get him home in time for his important business meeting the following morning.

They were down to five players and Huleo had less then an hour to make his flight. He quickly calculated the chips of the other players in comparison to his holdings. He still had far more then double anyone else's holdings. The antes where quickly rising, and most of the players would not last but a few more hands before they were out of the game. But he didn't have that kind of time to wait. He had a plane to catch.

He brilliantly threw an offer on the table to the remaining four players. Since he was so far ahead of everyone else, he would have been considered the favorite to win the tournament if it weren't for the fact that he had only an hour before he had to catch his plane. Of course, the others didn't know this. In what seemed like a benevolent move, he offered to take second place and let the four of them split up the rest. Since they were all hanging on by a thread and would most likely have been eliminated after a few more hands, they willingly agreed.

Had they known he was under such a time constraint they may not have been so agreeable. Huleo quickly collected his winnings and rushed to the airport only to find long lines going through security. No one was willing to let him go ahead of them. But his good fortune would continue to prevail. He made it to his flight just before they closed the door.

Had he known in advance that he was in a "lucky time" and that the stars were aligned for him when he ventured out to Vegas on his life-long dream trip, would he have done anything different? Maybe he would have played his cards differently, or maybe not. Maybe it was good that he didn't know. And maybe he would have booked a fight for the next day and not scheduled an important business meeting the day after the tournament.

So, what was going on in his chart? For those of you who are astrologically knowledgeable, you will find this to be very interesting. It just so happens that there was a solar eclipse that took place that very morning that coincided with the same degree as his natal Venus and Mars. Venus is the ruler of his 2nd house, which is related to his money and values, while Mars is the planet that is known for aggression and taking charge. Huleo certainly took action and took charge of his finances. And to make it even more interesting, Jupiter, the planet of expansion and optimism was entering his 2nd house of finances. So he had the confidence to make a deal with the other players. Whatever area of your life Jupiter is traveling though is usually thought to be beneficial unless there is some other negative aspect counteracting it.

The lesson of this story is you don't have to know anything about astrology—or even believe in it—for it to work. It has a system and energy all its own. And it is always working.

"Find the now and you'll find the shot"

~ Deepak Chopra

Chapter Eighteen
Golf Anyone?
A Game of Personalities

(You don't have to be a golfer to appreciate how the varied personalities found on a golf course interact. But if you are a golfer, I think you will really enjoy this chapter.)

I was almost a senior citizen when my interest in golf was sparked. I attribute this to meeting my husband, Tony. Not only did he love to play golf when I met him, but he enjoyed going to the PGA tournaments, as well as watching them on TV. I quickly saw that if this relationship was going to evolve into anything permanent, I could easily become a golf widow.

So, out of self defense, I began taking lessons. Golf lessons became a great Christmas and birthday gift, as Tony was only too eager to have me learn the game so we could play together when we went on vacation.

Now I love to play golf. But unfortunately I never seem

145

to have enough leisure time to play as much or as well as I would like. Golf is a game that requires anywhere from four to five hours to play, unless you are a pro or scratch golfer, in which case you could run through a course in half that time. But when the course is crowded, it doesn't matter much how good a player you are; you are going to do some waiting on the tee box.

For the average duffer like me, you're looking at taking the better part of a day. Then there's lunch with the girls afterwards. In some cases that's the best part of the day.

This crazy game, where you hit this little white ball until you get it in this little hole that is anywhere from fifty-five to five hundred yards away, can be a very social and entertaining way to spend your day. Or it can be a miserable, frustrating, exasperating experience. It can bring out the worst in a person or it can be relaxing and enjoyable.

One thing is certain. If you want to see someone's true personality, play a round of golf with them. Golf really does bring out the worst and best in people. It is a game of honesty, integrity, patience and precision. And of course it requires a great deal of practice and commitment.

So why do so many normal, average people spend so much of their leisure time and expendable income on this addictive sport? Beats me, but we do.

Statistics show that fifty-six million people play golf in the United States. I found that to be pretty amazing, considering that it is a rather expensive activity that requires specific equipment, lessons and greens fees, not to mention the time it takes to play a round of golf.

After many years of playing and observing others playing golf, I have come to some interesting conclusions. Golf is an art, not a science. We each approach the game in a different manner depending upon our individual personality. Since astrology is the study of personalities based on when a person is born and where the planets were at the time of their birth, this information can also be helpful on the golf course.

One other thing that this research has taught me is that age has no boundaries in the world of golf. Age is truly a state of mind and golf can keep you in a young state of mind. It keeps you active and involved in living. It doesn't matter if you are eight or eighty years old. The thrill of sinking that putt is the same. As someone once said, "we have to get old, but we don't have to act old."

All things being equal—like a person's skill level and ability—there are other factors to consider in predicting the outcome when playing golf. First what is the golfer's innate disposition? Is he or she easy going, competitive, high-spirited, or just having a bad day? Personality is another word for "innate disposition," so once again astrology has something to say.

GOLF IS A GAME OF ATTITUDE

Don't let your golf game dictate your attitude. Let your attitude dictate your game.

Have you ever noticed how much your golf game is affected by the weather? If it is raining or the course is wet you may believe that you won't strike the ball as well, and therefore you don't. Since most of us do not play golf for a living, we have the luxury of choosing the weather and conditions that we want to play in. A lot of us prefer not to play when it's too cold or too hot. We prefer the temperature and weather to be just right.

But what about our state of mind and attitude when we do play? It has been my observation and experience that this also plays a major factor in our performance. To paraphrase what Hall of Fame golfer Bobby Jones once said, golf is a game of inches, and the most important ones are the six inches that lie between your ears. Others have said the game is ninety percent mental, and the more I played the more I realized how true that is. For instance, most golfers know that when you hit a certain club well a few times in a row you start to expect you'll hit that club well. When you hit a club poorly a few times you can be defeated from the moment you pull it out of your bag.

A golfer who can keep his or her mind focused in the moment—with no past to haunt them and no grand hope for the future—has the best chance of striking the ball as planned. I have even used hypnosis and meditation to help improve my game.

I've enjoyed several of Bob Rotella's books, which focus on the mental aspect of golf, and found them to be very helpful. In his book, *Putting Out Of Your Mind,* he says, "If you're putting, you'll make your best stroke and hole the most putts if you think only of your target."

If we could all putt like young children we could probably take ten to fifteen strokes off our score. I asked my grandson one time when he was about four years old what he thought about when he was putting. He said, "I think about the ball going in, going in the hole." My thought was, *"of course, why didn't I think of that!"*

It has been my observation that in addition to a person's Sun sign affecting their golf personality, they are also affected by the position of the planets on the specific day that they are playing golf. This is called transiting planets. For example, I can recall playing one of my better rounds of golf when Mars, the planet that rules your physical energy and spirit of competition was traveling over my Sun.

Mars was acting as an energizer and thereby supporting the physical activity that I was engaged in that day. There were several other supporting transits which made the day very enjoyable. I actually won first place that day.

Attitude plays such a major role in your golf game that anything that affects the way you feel physically or mentally will also affect your game. So when you are having a bad round of golf, remember the planets just may not be lined up for you to produce your desired results.

There is another very interesting factor to be considered when playing golf. Not only are we influenced by the elements, but we are affected by the people we are playing with. It takes a strong constitution and mind to block out the chatter and attitude of the person who is sitting next to you in the golf cart, especially if you don't realize that it is affecting your game.

"I'VE ALWAYS THOUGHT IT WOULD BE INTERESTING TO ASSIGN FOURSOME PAIRINGS ACCORDING TO COMPATIBLE SUN SIGN PERSONALITIES."

Most golfers have noticed that some people can help lift your game up and others can pull your game down. The Executive Women's Golf Association that I belong to includes players with a variety of shapes, sizes, ages and Sun signs. This assortment has given me a vast range of personalities to observe on the golf course. I've always thought it would be interesting to assign pairings according to compatible Sun sign personalities. For those of you who are not golfers, "pairings" is the foursome you are assigned to when playing in a golf league.

But no matter who you are paired with, a good understanding of your own personality—meaning your Sun sign and astrology chart—can help you to better deal with distractions when you find yourself in a grouping that is not ideal for you.

THE GOLFER PERSONALITY

Aries – March 21 to April 20. They like to arrive at the course early, long before their tee time. They will always be the first one ready on the tee box. They like to be first to tee off and can become impatient with slow play. They may have difficulty following their ball as they are already thinking about their next shot and heading for the cart as soon as they complete their swing.

They especially enjoy the competition of the game. When it comes to putting, it would be beneficial for them to slow down and learn to focus on visioning the ball going into the hole. They can be aggressive and competitive players. They usually prefer playing with men rather than women. They do not mind and often prefer walking the course. They are not into small talk during their round, as they are always thinking about their next shot.

Taurus – April 21 to May 20. Slow moving and easy going Taurus will not be found rushing through their round of golf. Their slow easy swing can serve them well as they focus on their shot. They like to keep their attention focused on their game and do not like to be distracted with chatter and small talk.

Gemini – May 21 to June 20. They typically like to play at a rapid pace and can become agitated when the group ahead of them is playing slowly. This is especially true of the younger Gemini players. They are constantly tinkering with their swing and their club selection. They have a tendency to intellectualize their swing rather than allowing their subconscious to take over. They can be more conversational then some of the other Sun signs.

Cancer – June 21 to July 20. They will want to make you feel comfortable when you are playing with them. They will usually have food with them and are very willing to share. Since Cancers typically have more of a domestic nature, they are not usually found on the golf course. They are not known to be the athletic or outdoor type. They are comfort creatures and riding around all day in a golf cart may not be their cup of tea.

Leo – July 21 to August 20. They enjoy recognition and praise and playing golf is no exception. They enjoy the fun of the game and it is especially fun for them when they are winning. They can be risk takers and will go for the long shot rather than playing it safe. They don't mind and usually enjoy putting a few dollars on the game. They can be a lot of fun to play with, especially when they exhibit their entertaining nature.

Virgo – August 21 to September 20. These are the methodical, analytical golfers who enjoy following the rules of golf to the tee. They feel that everyone should do the same. After all, isn't golf about rules and regulations? They can become very upset if the game is not played properly. You may even find them making notes about their various club selections. They feel this is helpful to them for future reference.

They are the worker bees and backbone of any organization they belong to, be it a golf association or the PTA. They are inspired and motivated to perfect their game and can become very discouraged if their progress is not consistent. It is very important for them not to be too critical of themselves and those they play with. Less worry and more fun should be their motto. Golf is supposed to an enjoyable game.

Libra – September 21 to October 20. These are the diplomats and peacemakers on the golf course. You will never see them throwing their clubs or getting upset over a missed shot. They tend to be fairly easy going and a pleasure to play with. They have a slow and easy, rhythmic swing. They appear to be in balance and harmony all the time. Their quiet, soft demeanor can be a comfort when their playing partner is having a tough day staying out of the rough. Their easy going temperament is a complement and asset to their game.

Scorpio – October 21 to November 20. They will be quiet and deep in thought during their round of golf. They tend to internalize their emotions and feelings while they are playing. You rarely will see them blow up on the golf course. Most of the time, their expression will not reveal if they have hit a fantastic or disastrous shot. They are private by nature and carry this through to the course.

Sagittarius – November 21 to December 20. Since these are the gypsies of the zodiac, they enjoy playing golf around the world if possible. They've never met a new golf course that they didn't like. Their love of the outdoors makes golf a perfect outlet for their enthusiasm. They do not have to be a good golfer to enjoy the fresh air and open spaces. They are continuously analyzing and working on their swing. Their DVD library is up-to-date with numerous golf instructors' versions of "how to improve your game." This satisfies their love for analyzing their swing. After all, golf is a journey for them with no final destination. They are continually seeking new courses and their perfect swing. Their love of being outdoors in the fresh air is a significant factor in their attraction to the game.

Capricorn – December 21 to January 20. Their structured discipline serves them well on the golf course. They are the organized golfers. They are good at course management. They play their best rounds and are most comfortable when they pay attention to the shape and yardage of each hole and plan a strategy to get them to the green. They are frequently the leader of any organization of which they may be a member, or the leader in their foursome scramble. They usually prefer driving the golf cart rather then being a passenger.

Aquarius – January 21 to February 20. They enjoy the social aspect of the game. They prefer playing with friends and people they like. They enjoy belonging to golf clubs and organizations. It is truly a social outlet for them. They often will approach the game with a unique outlook many other golfers wouldn't understand, and usually do not take the game too seriously.

Pisces – February 22 to March 21. They can be easily influenced and affected by the people they are playing with. It is important for them to maintain a positive, upbeat attitude during their game. They have the ability to play golf from within, from a subconscious level. Once they have learned the mechanics, they can let their subconscious take over. They can get very down on themselves when they are not having a good round or playing up to, or better than, their handicap. They do not like to be responsible for keeping the score for the foursome.

Now that you understand a little more about your

golf personality you may want to think about which of the other personalities you feel most comfortable with and are most likely to enjoy playing with. After all, when you are playing with a compatible person your own game is usually better and more enjoyable.

"Success depends on where intention is."
~ Gita Bellin

CHAPTER NINETEEN

OF MONEY AND CAREER
SWIMMING WITH THE CURRENT

Most people know what their Sun sign is. They've read something in the newspaper or a magazine about their Sun sign. So they are a little familiar with the concept that when they were born might relate to their personality traits. But did you know that when we were born can affect our attitude about our finances, our security, the type of investments we are interested in and the type of investments that we are good at making money in?

Did you know that your astrology chart will also indicate if you are likely to loose money through fraud or poor judgment in your investment decisions? Yes, we have probably all had poor judgment in our investment decisions at one time or another, but some people are much more prone to doing that than others. And these traits can all be seen in your astrology chart.

Your astrology chart is the map that shows your financial potential and your attitude about money. It's sort of like looking at your financial DNA. Are you going to inherit a family fortune or will you need to earn your money like most of us have had to do. Perhaps you will marry into money or win your fortune.

Whichever is the case, your astrology chart will clarify your area of expertise and the type of work that you are most suited to do—or not do.

Although we cannot control or change what the stock market does, we can change our attitude about it. Do you have the personality or disposition to even be in the stock market? What level of volatility can we comfortably handle?

You can take better care of yourself financially if you understand your financial temperament. What investments are you comfortable with and what investments keep you awake at night? What is your risk comfort level? Some people like to invest in the stock market because they like the thrill. It's like going to Vegas. I have a sister-in-law who is like that. She likes the risky stocks that are very volatile. She watches them go up and she watches them go down, and she is usually very good at timing the buy and sell so that she makes a profit. But not everyone has that emotional temperament.

> "WHY SWIM UPSTREAM WHEN YOUR ASTROLOGY CHART IS INDICATING THAT YOU SHOULD TURN AROUND AND SWIM WITH THE CURRENT?"

Some people like the slow steady investment. They like the ones that pay interest or dividends without losing their principle. They don't need to make it all in one shot.

Many people are not of the disposition to invest for themselves, in which case they should select a financial planner or advisor that has a temperament and personality that is compatible with theirs. And some people do not have the resources to invest, but they invest their time and energy in their work.

IS IT WORK OR IS IT PLAY?

Have you ever asked yourself what type of work you are really passionate about? What are you really good at doing? Your astrology chart serves as the complete DNA map to all of this information.

For example, people who were born with their Sun in the sign of Taurus, Virgo and Capricorn are typically much more security oriented than those who were born with their Sun in the sign of Aries, Leo or Sagittarius. Here's a brief summary:

FIRE SIGNS – ARIES, LEO, SAGITTARIUS
(To review the elements, see page XII)

Aries, Leo and Sagittarius are Sun signs associated with being a risk taker. They enjoy having a certain amount of freedom and latitude in their chosen profession. They are not comfortable when they are tied down or locked into a routine job.

They like to speculate, and can get bored doing the same job all of the time. They can be impatient with their investments, so they will take risks in order to get a higher return. They are more comfortable doing that than a Taurus, Virgo or Capricorn would be.

Aries prefer to be self-employed and independent. They can work on commission and they can become bored with a repetitive job. Their interests may vary greatly and cause them to have more than one career path. They are initiators and are great with start-up businesses.

Sagittarius enjoys space, freedom and independence and the outdoors. Their line of work should afford them travel and versatility. They usually excel in sales position and interacting with people.

They love to take risks and usually tend to be lucky with investments. But they need to be careful or it can be "easy come easy go." They need to stash a reserve in a sock or under their mattress. They shouldn't put all of their eggs in one basket.

Think **Leo** and entertainers and risk takers come to mind. Manual labor does not suit their personality. They are often found in the performing arts.

They also are known for their warm charismatic personalities and charming ways. They enjoy being out front and center stage, and their career path should afford them this. They can be, and need to be, very creative in their work. They like to spend money on pretty things and have a taste for luxury. They tend to be very generous with their money.

EARTH SIGNS – TAURUS, VIRGO, CAPRICORN

People who were born with their Sun in Taurus, Virgo or Capricorn are more financially conservative. They are not likely to be risk takers. They like a sure thing. They do not overextend themselves financially.

It is important for them to have money in the bank. They need a backup plan, and they usually tend to be frugal and practical in managing their money.

Taurus's financial decisions are typically conservative and thrifty. It is not unusual to find them working in commerce or finances. In their personal life, they believe in saving for a rainy day. They enjoy shopping for a good bargain. They often stay with the same job or career for many years.

Virgos love being helpful and needed, which often draws them into service oriented professions. They can often be found working in the health or hospitality industry. Their attention to detail can also draw them to analytical and detail work.

Their propensity for monitoring even the smallest details often carries over to their finances. They are good at bookkeeping, so balancing their check book is a piece of cake. They don't make financial decisions quickly. They like to have all of the particulars in order first.

Capricorns are the captains of industry. They often will work in big business, or better yet, start and run their own business. They tend to resonate best when their work is structured and organized. They do not like to take financial risks and will avoid speculating. They can do well in real estate or working for the government.

AIR SIGNS – GEMINI, LIBRA, AQUARIUS

Gemini, Libra and Aquarius will frequently be involved in some sort of communications work. Their chosen career can involve writing, speaking, and/or public relations.

A **Gemini** will oftentimes have more than one source of income. They are not always good with managing their money. It is good for them to have help in this area. Balancing the check book is not their forte.

Libras are known for their skills at being a peace maker. They aspire to fight for justice. They are often lawyers, diplomats or counselors. They are tactful, charming and sociable. They prefer interaction with people in their careers, as opposed to working alone.

They usually display good financial judgment, probably because it takes them awhile to make up their mind before they spend money. They tend to be temperate and moderate in their finances, and are unlikely to do anything too extreme. Balance is important to them.

Aquarians are often entrepreneurial. I can recall one of my Aquarius clients who has started and sold two different unique businesses. Aquarians are typically very computer savvy. They are known for being innovators and idea people. They are also drawn to humanitarian work and become involved in groups and organizations.

WATER SIGNS – CANCER, SCORPIO, PISCES

Cancer, Scorpio and Pisces are the intuitive, sensitive signs of the zodiac. They feel most satisfied when their chosen work allows them to tap into their natural instincts.

Cancers are security oriented. They are not comfortable taking a risk. They prefer the tried and true, proven path.

They can be a gifted interior designer, a shopkeeper, or run a family business, like a "mom and pop" operation. A bed and breakfast is a good example. They can be a strong asset in a business setting, but they especially excel and enjoy their parenting role.

Scorpios are known for their critical, concentrated focus on their work. They are great at investigating or researching the facts. They can be private and secretive. Their chosen career path might be a paralegal, lawyer, chemist, emergency room technician, parapsychologist or psychologist.

They are private and conservative with their finances, so no one really knows very much about them. But be assured that whatever they invest in will be well researched.

Pisces' love of music can be seen in their personal and professional lives. Their chosen career can lead them to be a composer, ballet dancer, poet, impressionist painter, photographer, physician or antique dealer. They enjoy working behind the scenes rather then being in the limelight like a Leo would.

They are typically not good money managers, as they prefer to deal more with the abstract rather than the concrete.

Now that you have a general idea of your financial personality, how are you measuring up? Have you ever felt stuck in the wrong career or investments? Too much risk perhaps, and not enough reward? Even when we are in the wrong work—or wrong investments—we often persevere and manage to grin and bear it. But why swim upstream when your astrology chart is indicating that you should turn around and swim with the current?

"Each day comes bearing its own gifts.
Untie the ribbons."

~ Ruth Ann Schabacker

CHAPTER TWENTY

THE JOURNEY CONTINUES

IT'S BETTER TO GIVE THAN TO RECEIVE

I've always been taught that it is better to give than to receive. I can remember the excitement and the thrills I felt waiting for my parents to open their gift from me on Christmas morning or their birthdays. Of course, I loved the gifts that I received just as much. I still do for that matter, but I also still enjoy seeing the look of pleasure on a loved one's face when they open your gift and then smile back at you with a heartfelt "thank you."

My grandson learned at a very early age the thrill of giving a gift. I don't recall anyone ever teaching him that. In fact I don't know if that feeling can be taught. I can re-call how my heart melted one Christmas morning when he anxiously implored me to open *his* present to me first. His eyes sparkled and gleamed as I opened his beautifully wrapped Christmas present. I could hardly keep from crying as I read the inscription on the bottom of his handmade, personalized pottery breadbasket. It read, "To Grand-ma-ma, Love Breck." I could see the happiness in his little six-year-old eyes as he watched his grand-ma-ma open her special gift that he had spent months making.

I also felt this same happiness when my sister gave me the most exquisite Vera Bradley purse that I had ever seen. Although she was not six years old, she still had that gleam in her eyes as she watched me open her very special gift to me. We are never too old or too young to enjoy giving and receiving gifts. And some gifts just keep on giving, like the joy that I feel when I work with my clients.

Gifts come in many forms

I have always considered myself very fortunate to have worked in jobs that I enjoyed. I always felt that I was making a difference or contribution in whatever job I was doing. Because I knew that it was "in the stars" for me to live a structured and organized life, work and a career have always felt very satisfying for me. I feel extremely blessed and fortunate to have been led to the path of astrology.

One of the first things that I learned when I was studying astrology is that there are many branches in the field of astrology, just as there are specialized branches in government or medicine. There is mundane astrology, natural astrology, horary astrology, medical astrology, financial astrology, electional astrology and AstroLocality astrology

Some astrologists specialize in one area or another. Mundane astrology, for instance, covers everything which is not personal or doesn't deal with a personal chart. Some of the things that are considered to be mundane are political events and the chart of a nation or a business. It can be used to predict the outcome of an election, or the fate and temperament of a nation. Another specialized form, horary astrology, is based on casting a chart for the moment in time that a question is asked. For example a person may ask the question, "Where did I loose my diamond tennis bracelet?" To an experienced trained astrologer in this field, the chart would help reveal the answer. AstroLocality astrology can be used to pick a good place to live, or to vacation, or to attract clients for your business. Medical astrology is used to help detect the part of the body that may be prone to weakness or illness.

> "MY FAVORITE MEMORIES AS AN ASTROLOGY COUNSELOR OFTEN INVOLVE HAPPY ENDINGS FOR CLIENTS WITH WHOM I'VE WORKED FOR MANY YEARS."

Although I have an understanding of these specialized areas, and occasionally help clients in these pursuits, most of my work as an astrological counselor focuses on the day-to-day concerns of real-world people. The main emphasis is on relationships, romance, finances, and timing.

The branch of astrology that deals with selecting the best time to initiate any given activity or project is called electional astrology. It can involve anything from listing your house for sale to planning your wedding date. It can help select a date to start your dream vacation, schedule elective surgery, or ask for a raise. Since the time at which an event begins sets a pattern in motion, it is important to select the best available time for the most desirable outcome.

This is by far and without a doubt my most favorite area of astrology. I have worked extensively over the years with helping clients plan just the right time to begin an event or take an anticipated action. I find this to be extremely helpful in my personal as well as professional life. It's nice to be able to look back in time and learn from our successes and failures, but it is invaluable to be able to plan for the future.

APPRECIATION AND ATTRACTION

The longer I live, the more I appreciate how much I have to be thankful for. I feel so fortunate that my life journey and my final chosen career path have led me to where I am today. It is everything and more than I could have hoped for when I first began my studies thirty years ago.

Of course, astrological counseling is a business. That is the nature of being a professional, whatever your field. But when I think of the clients I've served over the years, I see them as beautiful gifts generously given to me—gifts more beautiful than I ever could have imagined. I never knew when the next gift would arrive, or where it would come from. But somehow they came, and so often clients became friends. Looking back, I still couldn't explain how they found me or how I found them; it just always seemed to happen.

Another thing I began to notice as my experience grew was that whenever I was going through a crisis or a transition in my life, I always seemed to attract clients who were going through the same situations. For example, I can recall that during the time immediately after my former husband passed away, several clients were suddenly referred to me who were in the same situation.

There have been long periods in my life when I was single. During those times I attracted many, many clients who were also single and looking for Mr. or Ms. Right. Of course, none of them knew anything about what was happening in my life when they made their appointment.

Some might say it's not unusual, especially in Florida, for people to have a spouse pass on, or to be single and seeking a mate. And it's not unusual for me to get new clients. But what seems to be numerically unusual is to have a series of clients turning to me for help, all of them sharing the same transitory moment in life that I am experiencing. It has happened time and again, in many different ways. Purely coincidental? Some would say, of course. But the longer I live and the more I see, the deeper my understanding becomes that coincidences are truly rare.

I mentioned in an earlier chapter that I was originally drawn to astrology because it is more concrete than other metaphysical practices and not so dependent on the mind of the practitioner. But having said that, I must add that not all astrology counselors are equal. A lot depends on the counselor's skills, empathy and experience. Life is full of experiences and the more we have and live through (hopefully we live through them), the more we can understand and relate to others when they are going through a similar life experience and crisis. A counselor who understands life in all its dimensions will bring insight to helping clients decide how to apply the information that is identified in their chart. And although it is not a "technical" requirement, an astrologer who feels genuine compassion is likely to form a stronger and longer-lasting bond with his or her clients.

FAMILY TIES

I am eternally grateful that astrology has helped me to better understand and appreciate my family and friends. For example, had it not been for astrology I would never have understood my Gemini son when he was growing up. It helped me to realize that it is perfectly normal and natural for a seven-year-old who is a Gemini to be able to watch TV, read a book and play a game all at the same time. This was long before cell phones and texting, or he would have been doing that too. And he did all of this very naturally with little effort and without thinking a thing about it. After all, isn't everyone multi-task oriented?

I also learned that my Virgo sister was the best friend in the world that a person could have. She always watched for her big sister. I could call her in the middle of the night for help and she would be there. As a matter of fact, I have called and she never complained.

I can recall when my son was born. It was the summer of her senior year in high school in Florida. My sister generously volunteered to spend the summer with me in North Carolina where we were living at the time. As sweet and precious as my son was, he was unfortunately one of these babies that liked to sleep all day and stay up all night. Since I wasn't one of those new mothers that bounced right back, I was eternally grateful for her help. A full night's sleep meant the world to me. My Virgo sister continues to be my soul support.

My Capricorn mother and Taurus father taught me the true meaning of being organized, structured and disciplined as I was growing up. I didn't get away with a thing. I always had to follow the rules, which was not an easy task for a little Aries girl. My 84-year-old mother is still the most organized person that I know.

Life is Good — A happy ending

My favorite memories as an astrology counselor often involve happy endings for clients with whom I've worked for many years. I keep a warm spot in my heart for a client I met at the dude ranch I mentioned earlier, where I worked as astrological counselor to the guests during the early stages of my career. Abigail was in her mid-thirties when we first met. She had never been married. She always seemed to attract men who where emotionally unavailable. Although she said that she wanted to get married, the men to whom she was attracted were not good candidates to support that agenda. She was shopping on the wrong aisle of life's supermarket.

Abigail would schedule an appointment with me about twice a year to discuss what was going on with her current love interest. I could see from her astrology chart that her long-standing love fascination was going nowhere fast at that time. The fact that he lived on the other side of the country certainly didn't help the situation. But the bottom line was that he was just emotionally unavailable, period.

So, over our time together we worked through that relationship and finally saw it end. Then, over the next few years we watched several more relationships come and go. And then, bingo! She actually met Mr. Right. As was her practice, she called with his birth information and we set up an appointment to discuss the potential compatibility.

I couldn't have been more excited for her if this had been happening to me personally. Her new friend appeared to be a refreshing change from the type of men that she had been attracting in the past. Although they lived in different cities, the hundred mile separation was nowhere near the challenge the three thousand mile relationship had been.

Within a year and just before the market crash— timing is everything —she sold her house and moved in with him. Neither of them was interested in starting a family so there was no rush to tie the knot. They enjoyed traveling; they both had their careers. Life was good.

As the stars would have it, marriage was to be in their future. At age fifty-three she was going to marry for the first time. She had met her Prince Charming and I felt honored to have been consulted to help them select their wedding date.

They eventually moved from his place and built a beautiful home together where they are living happily ever after. Life is good. I always love a happy ending.

Information and Inspiration

My clients come to me with many different situations, challenges and aspirations. They come from many different parts of the country and the world, but everyone is basically looking for the same things: information and inspiration.

It's easy to fall into believing that a truly inspired life is something reserved for a very small group. But through the use of astrology it's been my pleasure to help many people see that we all can live like that. I personally find inspiration in being able to observe the movement of the planets in relation to what is going on in our lives and how long it will last. It's a lot easier to handle a difficult cycle when you can see the light at the end of the tunnel. And how wonderful it is to prepare for and look forward to those uplifting and positive planetary cycles.

Life is a journey and with the help and understanding that have come to me through astrology, the past thirty years have been a much more enjoyable journey for me.

*"Peace of mind comes from not wanting to change others,
but by simply accepting them as they are.
True acceptance is always without demands and expectations."*

Gerald G. Jampolsky, *Love is Letting Go of Fear*

CHAPTER TWENTY-ONE

MY LIFE WITH THE STARS

LET THE WIND FILL YOUR SAILS

I can still vividly remember those days when I felt that I was adrift—the proverbial sailboat without a rudder. And worse yet, I had no understanding of why I felt so lost. My astrological journey has served me well. It has been a reliable and stable influence in my life. And it has allowed me to be a reliable and stable influence for my family, friends and clients.

Gone are the days when I felt uncertain about my direction in life and my feelings. I hope my words have expressed what a privilege it's been to share my gains with others. When someone comes to a "professional" for help—whether it's with their car, their plumbing or their relationship—they are looking for someone in whom they can place their trust and confidence, not someone they sense is flying by the seat of their pants. Much of that self-assurance comes from experience. There is no way in life to escape the learning curve.

Fortunately, I have come to a place in my life where I can meet my clients from a position of strength and confidence, without forgetting the trials I have endured in my own journey. I can empathize and appreciate when someone comes to me with a life challenging or an all-consuming personal problem, because I too have gone through many of these same challenges. Before astrology, my challenges seemed to be unmanageable and overwhelming. Through the help of understanding the movement of the planets and how they affect us on earth, life's challenges have been pared down from mountains to foothills.

Throughout the years I have developed and maintained an astrology newsletter for my clients and friends. My desire in creating the newsletter was to help my clients stay in touch with what is going on in the heavens on a monthly basis. I have enjoyed sharing this gift every month and especially enjoy the gift I receive when clients email me their comments about how this information has helped them and been useful in their daily lives.

Knowledge can bring peace. My astrological journey has brought me peace. It has enabled me to share my experiences and my tools—and my love for people.

Using the cycles of the Moon to help plan and organize my life and my daily activities has been invaluable. I've seen the results and the outcome of good timing and planning over the years.

I've learned that we can take charge of our lives—that we aren't destined to be victims of the fickle hand of fate. I've leaned that achieving a desired outcome is truly a product of good planning and good timing.

And I've learned that it's OK to have non-productive days—days when you just want to hang out. Because the Moon—the planet that affects our emotions—continues to change as it moves through its phases, our moods also continue to change.

Sometimes all of life's changes can feel like a storm, but they don't need to. Look to the stars to understand where you are, where you've been, and what lies ahead. Then just relax, let the wind fill your sails, and enjoy the journey.

To continue enjoying your journey with Kelly Lowe, join her on her website, *www.astrologytalk.com*.
An Astrologer's Journey is available on the website.

CPSIA information can be obtained at www.ICGtesting.com
Printed in the USA
LVOW031022021111

253184LV00001B/4/P